Copyright © 1975 by Phyllis Hobe
First edition
Printed in the United States of America

Acknowledgment is gratefully made for:

"What Children Teach Us About Christmas," by Catherine
Marshall, *McCall's*, December, 1955.

Christmas card illustrations by William Blood, Franklin Elton-
head, Grace Norcross Fisher, John Geiszel, Margaret Malpass
Geiszel, H. Rudolph Pott, Aldred Scott, Marguerite Walter, and
Jessie Wissler.

U.S. Library of Congress Cataloging in Publication Data

Main entry under title:

The Meaning of Christmas.

    1. Christmas–Literary collections.   I. Hobe,
Phyllis.
PN6071.C6M42   808.8'033   75–12627
ISBN–0–87981–045–9

To John

Contents

Preface

Almost two thousand years ago, in a cave that served as a stable for a crowded inn in a congested city, a Child was born—and the world has never been the same. The event has changed people's lives, their customs, sensitivities, politics, allegiance, and even their destinies.

Each year people all over the world observe the significance of that birth. The anniversary of that moment has become our most important holiday. Joyfully, reverently, traditionally, in our own individual ways, we interrupt the routine and the busyness of our lives to reach out to the Child and find comfort in his coming.

Christmas is a very personal time, a time when the individual searches his faith for the deeper meaning of life. And because it is so personal, it means something different to each one of us. To some it's the delight of giving and the humility of receiving; to some it's the feasting, the celebrating, the gleam of the ornamented tree, the presence of friends and the gathering of families; to many it's the opportunity to regain a sense of wonder through the anticipation in the eyes of children; and for most it's the awakening of an abundant love for all persons, all creatures, everywhere.

In these pages many writers, past and present, express what Christmas means to them—and in these pages may the reader find words that will reach into his own heart to identify the beautiful feelings there.

Phyllis Hobe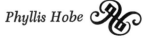

The
Meaning
of Christmas

The Season

CHRISTMAS GREETING

Sing hey! Sing hey!
For Christmas Day;
Twine mistletoe and holly,
For friendship glows
In winter snows,
And so let's all be jolly.
Author Unknown

OLD CHRISTMASTIDE

Heap on more wood!—the wind is chill;
But let it whistle as it will
We'll keep our Christmas merry still.
Sir Walter Scott

DEAR FRIEND

In the dull routine of living,
 Christmas comes once more to bring
A glow of warmth and friendliness
 to brighten everything . . .
And along with many millions
 who observe this joyful season,
I have come to think of Christmas
 as a most inspiring reason
To get in touch with dear old friends,
 time compels me to neglect,
As well as with acquaintances
 I admire and respect . . .
For in business and in pleasure,
 in fact, every place I go,
I am always meeting people who
 are so worthwhile to know . . .
And, because my days are crowded
 and my hours are too few,
I cannot keep in touch with them
 the way I'd like to do . . .
So this happy little habit
 that I indulge in yearly
Is just an indication
 that I'm wishing you sincerely
All the special blessings,
 all the peace and joy and love
That are yours just for the asking
 from OUR FATHER up above . . .
And while this selfsame message
 goes to many, it is true,
The words that you are reading
 were written "JUST FOR YOU" . . .
For whether you're an old friend,
 or someone I've just met,
A "stranger" only is a FRIEND
 I do not know, as yet . . .
And for everybody, everywhere,
 I pray this Christmas prayer:
"May the GOOD LORD BLESS US, EVERY ONE,
 and KEEP US IN HIS CARE."

Helen Steiner Rice

Christmas is the season for kindling the fire of hospitality in the hall, the genial flame of charity in the heart.

Washington Irving

I have always thought of Christmas time, when it has come round, as a good time; a kind, forgiving, charitable time; the only time I know of, in the long calendar of the year, when men and women seem by one consent to open their shut-up hearts freely, and to think of people below them as if they really were fellow passengers to the grave, and not another race of creatures bound on other journeys. ... And so as Tiny Tim said: "A merry Christmas to us all, my dears. God bless us, every one."

Charles Dickens

THE STORY OF THE GOBLINS WHO STOLE A SEXTON

In an old abbey town, a long, long while ago—so long, that the story must be a true one, because our great-grandfathers implicitly believed it—there was a sexton and gravedigger in the churchyard, one Gabriel Grub. It by no means follows that because a man is a sexton, and constantly surrounded by emblems of mortality, therefore he should be a morose and melancholy man; your undertakers are the merriest fellows in the world. But, Gabriel Grub was an ill-conditioned, cross-grained, surly fellow—a morose and lonely man, who consorted with nobody but himself and an old wicker bottle which fitted into his large deep waistcoat pocket.

A little before twilight, one Christmas Eve, Gabriel shouldered his spade, lighted his lantern, and betook himself toward the old churchyard; for he had got a grave to finish by next morning, and, feeling very low, he thought it might raise his spirits, perhaps, if he went on with his work at once.

Gabriel strode along until he turned into the dark lane which led to the churchyard. He had been looking forward to reaching the dark lane, because it was, generally speaking, a nice, gloomy, mournful place, into which the townspeople did not much care to go, except

16

in broad daylight and when the sun was shining; consequently, he was not a little indignant to hear a young urchin roaring out some joyful song about a merry Christmas in this very sanctuary.

Gabriel waited until the boy came up and then dodged him into a corner and rapped him over the head with his lantern, five or six times, to teach him to modulate his voice. And as the boy hurried away with his hand to his head, singing quite a different sort of tune, Gabriel Grub chuckled very heartily to himself, and entered the churchyard, locking the gate behind him.

He took off his coat, put down his lantern, and getting into the unfinished grave, worked at it for an hour or so with right good will. He was so well pleased with having stopped the small boy's singing, that he took little heed of the scanty progress he had made and looked down into the grave, when he had finished work for the night, with grim satisfaction; murmuring as he gathered up his things:

> "Brave lodgings for one, brave lodgings for one,
> A few feet of cold earth, when life is done,
> A stone at the head, a stone at the feet,
> A rich, juicy meal for the worms to eat:
> Rank grass over head, and damp clay around,
> Brave lodgings for one, these, in holy ground!"

"Ho! ho!" laughed Gabriel Grub, as he sat himself down on a flat tombstone, which was a favorite resting-place of his, and drew forth his wicker bottle, "A coffin at Christmas! A Christmas Box! Ho! ho! ho!"

"Ho! ho! ho!" repeated a voice which sounded close behind him.

Gabriel paused in some alarm, in the act of raising the wicker bottle to his lips, and looked around him. Not the faintest rustle broke the profound tranquility of the solemn scene. Sound itself appeared to be frozen up, all was so cold and still.

"It was the echoes," said Gabriel Grub, raising the bottle to his lips again.

"It was not," said a deep voice.

Gabriel started up, and stood rooted to the spot with astonishment and terror; for his eyes rested on a form that made his blood run cold.

Seated on an upright tombstone, close to him, was a strange, unearthly figure, whom Gabriel felt at once was no being of this world. His long fantastic legs, which might have reached the ground, were cocked up, and crossed after a quaint, fantastic fashion; his sinewy arms were bare; and his hands rested on his knees. On his short, round body he wore a close covering; a short cloak dangled at his back; and his shoes curled up at the toes into long points. On his head he wore a broad-brimmed sugar-loaf hat, garnished with a single feather. The hat was covered with the white frost; and the goblin looked as if he had sat on the same tombstone very comfortably for two or three hundred years. He was sitting perfectly still; his tongue was put out, as if in derision; and he was grinning at Gabriel Grub with such grin as only a goblin could call up.

"It was not the echoes," said the goblin.

Gabriel Grub was paralyzed, and could make no reply.

"What man wanders among the graves and churchyards on such a night as this?" cried the goblin.

"Gabriel Grub! Gabriel Grub!" screamed a wild chorus of voices that seemed to fill the churchyard. Gabriel looked fearfully round—nothing was to be seen.

"What have you got in that bottle?" said the goblin.

"Hollands, sir," replied the sexton, trembling more than ever; for he had bought it of the smugglers and he thought that perhaps his questioner might be in the excise department of the goblins.

"Who drinks Hollands alone, and in a churchyard, on such a night as this?" said the goblin.

"Gabriel Grub! Gabriel Grub!" exclaimed the wild voices again.

The goblin leered maliciously at the terrified sexton, and then raising his voice, exclaimed:

"And who, then, is our fair and lawful prize?"

To this inquiry the invisible chorus replied, "Gabriel Grub! Gabriel Grub!"

"What do you think of this, Gabriel?" said the goblin, kicking his dead feet in the air on either side of the tombstone.

"It's—it's—very curious, sir," replied the sexton, half dead with fright. "Very curious, and very pretty, but I think I'll go back and finish my work, sir, if you please."

"Work!" said the goblin; "what work?"

"The grave, sir; making the grave," stammered the sexton.

"Oh, the grave, eh?" said the goblin. "Who makes graves at a time of night when all other men are merry, and takes a pleasure in it?"

Again the mysterious voices replied, "Gabriel Grub! Gabriel Grub!"

"I'm afraid my friends want you, Gabriel," said the goblin.

"Under favor, sir," replied the horror-stricken sexton, "I don't think they can, sir; they don't know me, sir; I don't think the gentlemen have ever seen me, sir."

"Oh, yes, they have," replied the goblin. "We know the man with the sulky face and the grim scowl. We know the man who struck the boy in the envious malice of his heart, because the boy could be merry and he could not. We know him, we know him."

Here the goblin gave a loud shrill laugh, which the echoes returned twentyfold. "I—I—am afraid I must leave you, sir," said the sexton, making an effort to move.

"Leave us!" said the goblin, "Gabriel Grub is going to leave us. Ho! ho! ho!"

Suddenly darting toward him, he laid his hand upon his collar, and sank with him through the earth.

When Gabriel Grub had had time to fetch his breath, which the rapidity of his descent had for the moment taken away, he found himself in what appeared to be a large cavern, surrounded on all sides by crowds of goblins, ugly and grim; in the center of the room, on an elevated seat, was stationed his friend of the churchyard; and close beside him stood Gabriel Grub himself, without the power of motion.

"Cold tonight," said the king of the goblins, "very cold. A glass of something warm, here!"

At this command, half-a-dozen officious goblins, with a perpetual smile upon their faces, whom Gabriel Grub imagined to be courtiers, on that account, hastily disappeared, and presently returned with a goblet of liquid fire, which they presented to the king.

"Ah!" cried the goblin, whose cheeks and throat were transparent, as he tossed the flame down, "this warms one, indeed! Bring a bumper of the same for Mr. Grub."

It was in vain for the unfortunate sexton to protest that he was not in the habit of taking anything warm at night; one of the goblins held him while another poured the blazing liquid down his throat; the whole assembly screeched with laughter as he coughed and choked, and wiped away the tears which gushed plentifully from his eyes, after swallowing the burning draught.

"And now," said the king, fantastically poking the tapered corner of his sugar-loaf hat into the sexton's eye, and thereby occasioning him the most exquisite pain; "and now show the man of misery and gloom a few of the pictures from our great storehouse!"

As the goblin said this, a thick cloud which obscured the remoter end of the cavern rolled gradually away and disclosed, apparently at a great distance, a small and scantily furnished, but neat and clean apartment. A crowd of little children were gathered round a bright fire, clinging to their mother's gown and gamboling around her chair. The mother occasionally rose and drew aside the window-curtain, as if to look for some expected object; a frugal meal was already spread upon the table; and an elbow-chair was placed near the fire. A knock was heard from the door, and the children crowded round her as she opened the door, clapping their hands for joy as their father entered. He was wet and weary, and shook the snow from his garments, as the

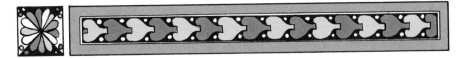

children crowded round him, and seizing his cloak, hat, stick, and gloves, with busy zeal, ran with them from the room. Then, as he sat down to his meal before the fire, the children climbed about his knee, and the mother sat by his side, and all seemed happiness and comfort.

But a change came upon the view almost imperceptibly. The father and mother were old and helpless now, and the number of those about them was diminished more than half; but content and cheerfulness sat on every face and beamed in every eye. Slowly and peacefully the father sank into the grave, and soon after, the sharer of all his cares and troubles followed him to a place of rest. The few who yet survived them knelt by their tomb and watered the green turf which covered it with their tears; then rose and turned away; sadly and mournfully, but not with bitter cries or despairing lamentations, for they knew that they should one day meet again; and once more they mixed with the busy world, and their content and cheerfulness were restored. The cloud settled upon the picture and concealed it from the sexton's view.

"What do you think of that?" said the goblin, turning his large face toward Gabriel Grub.

Gabriel murmured out something about its being very pretty, and looked somewhat ashamed, as the goblin bent his fiery eyes upon him.

"*You* a miserable man!" said the goblin in a tone of excessive contempt. He lifted up one of his very pliable legs, and flourishing it above his head a little to insure his aim, administered a good sound kick to Gabriel Grub; immediately after which all the goblins in waiting crowded round the wretched sexton and kicked him without mercy; according to the established and invariable custom of courtiers upon earth, who kick whom royalty kicks, and hug whom royalty hugs.

"Show him some more!" said the king of the goblins.

Many a time the cloud went and came, and many a lesson it taught to Gabriel Grub, who, although his shoulders smarted with pain from the frequent applications of the goblins' feet, looked on with interest that nothing could diminish. He saw that men who worked hard and earned their scanty bread with lives of labor were cheerful and happy. He saw that women, the tenderest and most fragile of all God's creatures, were the oftenest superior to sorrow, adversity, and distress; and he saw that it was because they bore, in their own hearts, an inexhaustible well-spring of affection and devotion. Above all, he

saw that men like himself, who snarled at the mirth and cheerfulness of others, were the foulest weeds on the fair surface of the earth; and, setting all the good of the world against the evil, he came to the conclusion that it was a very decent and respectable sort of world, after all. No sooner had he formed it, than the cloud which had closed over the last picture seemed to settle on his senses and lull him to repose. One by one the goblins faded from his sight; and as the last one disappeared, he sunk to sleep.

The day had broken when Gabriel Grub awoke—and found himself lying at full length on the flat gravestone in the churchyard with the wicker bottle lying empty by his side and his coat, spade, and lantern, all well whitened by the last night's frost, scattered on the ground. The stone on which he had first seen the goblin seated stood bolt upright before him, and the grave at which he had worked, the night before, was not far off. At first, he began to doubt the reality of his adventures, but the acute pain in his shoulders when he attempted to rise assured him that the kicking of the goblins was certainly not ideal. So Gabriel Grub got on his feet as well as he could, for the pain in his back; and brushing the frost off his coat, put it on and turned his face toward the town.

But he was an altered man, and he could not bear the thought of returning to a place where his repentance would be scoffed at and his reformation disbelieved. He hesitated for a few moments; and then turned away to wander where he might and seek his bread elsewhere.

The lantern, the spade, and the wicker bottle were found, that day, in the churchyard. There were a great many speculations about the sexton's fate, at first, but it was speedily determined that he had been carried away by the goblins; and there were not wanting some very credible witnesses who had distinctly seen him whisked through the air on the back of a chestnut horse blind of one eye, with the hind-quarters of a lion, and the tail of a bear.

Unfortunately, these stories were somewhat disturbed by the unlooked-for reappearance of Gabriel Grub himself, some ten years afterward, a ragged, contented, rheumatic old man. He told his story to the clergyman and also to the mayor; and in course of time it began to be received, as a matter of history, in which form it has continued down to this very day.

Charles Dickens

BELLS ACROSS THE SNOW

O Christmas, merry Christmas!
  Is it really come again,
With its memories and greetings,
  With its joy and with its pain?
There's a minor in the carol,
  And a shadow in the light,
And a spray of cypress twining
  With the holly wreath to-night.
And the hush is never broken
  By laughter light and low,
As we listen in the starlight
  To the "bells across the snow."

O Christmas, merry Christmas!
  'Tis not so very long
Since other voices blended
  With the carol and the song!
If we could but hear them singing
  As they are singing now,
If we could but see the radiance
  Of the crown on each dear brow;
There would be no sigh to smother,
  No hidden tear to flow,
As we listen in the starlight
  To the "bells across the snow."

O Christmas, merry Christmas!
  This never more can be;
We cannot bring again the days
  Of our unshadowed glee.
But Christmas, happy Christmas,
  Sweet herald of good-will,
With holy songs of glory
  Brings holy gladness still.
For peace and hope may brighten,
  And patient love may glow,
As we listen in the starlight
  To the "bells across the snow."
                    Frances Ridley Havergal

CHRISTMAS ISLAND *

Quite by accident, just before Christmas in 1961, I found St. Simons Island off the coast of Georgia, and I've never been the same since. I live here now, a part of the landscape, warmly and intimately related to a community—more involved with people and problems to be solved than ever in my life. Far more aware of the fact of God than at any time during the years spent working off a speaking schedule no altogether sane person would tackle. Saner, quieter, thinking things through instead of tossing off glib answers—and they were often glib, I fear, in spite of my earnest intentions. Rushing madly from engagement to engagement could well have been God's idea for me during those first years of my life in Him. At least, He went along. But He is here, too, and demanding of me a deeper look at everything, a deeper responsibility to communicate His love in what I write and in the daily round.

I am thinking toward a book some day in which I may set down some of the ways living on an island—this island—has changed me. But in this one chapter, the change can be telescoped into Christmas on St. Simons. When possible, in the years since my closest friend and fellow writer, Joyce Blackburn, and I discovered this little sandy strip of land while on a promotion tour for my book, *Beloved World*, I have spent Christmas here on what the developers are now calling "the innocent island." When we found it, St. Simons was indeed an innocent island . . . before the developers came.

Wide-branched live oaks, tall sweet gums, tupelos, pines and hickory trees sheltered quiet, shadow-streaked Frederica Road, the island's only north and south thoroughfare, and from early November through Christmas, ropes of yellow bullis and scuppernong grapevines twisted at random from the ground's lush undergrowth to the tops of these trees, just often enough intertwined with scarlet creeper. In late autumn and winter one can still drive up Frederica Road and find patches of this celebratory decoration, but only patches. Well-tended golf courses, tennis courts and condominiums stretch north now along the beloved road, and roadsides—once raucous with wildflowers and briary vines and brilliant sumac—are kept mowed to sterile neatness.

"We have to accommodate our new, heavy mowing machinery," the man explained at a meeting of the County Commission. "You can't mow with all those tough vines and cassina berries and marsh elder in the way of the new, wider machine!"

Red plumes of turkey grass, as festive as any Christmas table centerpiece, once waved along the marsh causeway and lit the shadows beside Frederica Road. "Got to spray chemicals in those drainage ditches," the muscled gentleman declared. "How we going to drain off those golf courses with the ditches clogged up? The way things grow here, it can't be done."

I'm sure he's right. And golf courses provide healthy, pleasant recreation for tired city folk who seek out our island. This is not a tirade against developers or well-manicured golf courses. It is a small remembering, held close to this day, of earlier Christmases on St. Simons Island when a long walk down Frederica Road also provided an unforgettable experience. Healthy, too, I suppose, if one could manage enough discipline to walk briskly. I never could. There was too much to look at—too many heart-shaped, golden grape leaves, too thick a growth of shiny smilax, too many poignantly beautiful small gifts from God for brisk walking. I always had to restrain myself from hugging it all, helped along in my restraint, of course, by the fact that red bugs (chiggers to Yankees) are often still around at Christmas in our mild climate. But a walk among the clean shadows thrown by the tall trees standing in the indescribable island light was once a worship experience. The traffic is too heavy now for a walk down Frederica Road.

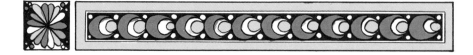

Some of us, the old-timers and a few outsiders who had been here, as we had, for several years, stayed ill for a while at what was happening to our wild places. Our conflict heightened because we had loved living here and it didn't seem right to want no one else to come. Almost overnight our large Concerned Citizens group sprang into being when a developer's plan for ringing Christ Church Frederica with paved roads and condominiums was submitted to the County Commission. Not historic old Christ Churchyard! After all, Joyce and I were here only because on that first discovery day we had seen this unbelievably romantic spot, and I had found a true story for my first novel, *The Beloved Invader*.

The dear little white Victorian church stands in its peaceful, still-untouched woods as of this writing, and we like to think our efforts to steer the population growth to a more appropriate direction helped bring about the change in the development plans. The original developer sold out to a more sensitive new one. The latest word is that the woods around Christ Church and Ft. Frederica National Park, where General James Oglethorpe defended the colony of Georgia from Spain, will be developed in single-family residences. This is fine. We live on the north end of the island, too, and if newcomers love it as we do and can tolerate the deer flies for half of each year, well and good. (After all, wearing a protective beekeeper's helmet to the mailbox or on a stroll around our winding shell lane is small penalty for the joy of living in the midst of such beauty and wildness.)

Years ago Joyce and I were fortunate enough to find a secluded point of land (nowhere available now) extending out into Sydney Lanier's Marshes of Glynn on three sides and sheltered by woods on the fourth. Much of the adjoining woods have now been pitiably thinned, but we cleared only space for our house and our own small woods still stand. We've stopped having them cleared at all. Let the snakes come. We'll just walk more carefully. We can keep at least what we own of the old St. Simons.

Let the smilax and the grapevines and the wild cassina and marsh elder grow rampant! Our hearts grow rampant with them. Most important—*we grow*.

Some understanding of what Jesus meant when he spoke of the lilies of the field, which grow just by standing there in place—meeting the conditions of growth—can be grasped, I suppose, by almost

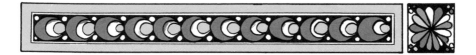

25

anyone. In large areas of my own life, I caught on to the value of quiet, resting faith even when I lived in the middle of a noisy metropolis. Living here, I've learned still more of what he must have meant.

Make no mistake, idyllic day does not follow silent, idyllic day on St. Simons Island. The air is often filled with the drone of private planes, and I work harder than ever before since I've begun writing long, difficult-to-research historical novels about the early days along America's southeastern coast. I find it harder to keep up with the increasing mail and outside requests—the eager tourists who arrive because they've liked my trilogy of novels laid here.

But I've come to see that the grapevines and the marsh elders grow and turn yellow or bloom white and feathery—*in silence*. The kind of searching silence that compels me to inner transactions with the living God who thought of them in the first place. The marshes stretch away—brown and green in summer, golden in autumn and winter, yellow green in spring—and only one glance out over their vast morning quietness when I open the shutters each day to check

the tide or the blue sky reflected in the nearby river turns me to God, even on the mornings when my mind had already begun to churn with the telephone calls and letters to write before I can begin work on whatever manuscript is current for that day.

One look at the quiet marshes brings the reminder of God, and that the earth *is* the Lord's. And the heart turns both inward and outward—inward toward the fact of his presence there in each person who believes that he *is* as Jesus Christ showed him to be. Outward toward his world—his hungry, lost, bomb-scarred, politically troubled world. The kind of outward turn which drives one to action, not only in prayer, but in deed.

Days lived close to the earth he created do not—at least, my experience is that they need not—turn one only inward. In spite of the anxieties of some of my longtime friends who prophesied that once I'd moved away from the big city and cut down the speaking dates, I'd become a selfish, do-not-disturb-me recluse, the opposite has happened. Yes, I do have to keep my Georgia farm gate locked and posted with (I hope) a polite sign informing that "uninvited guests cannot be received." This is only because I now live in a resort area where tourists, bless them, who have read my trilogy of St. Simons novels drive up to my gate in droves—just to shake my hand. I wish I could shake every hand. But inevitably the traveler is on vacation, with time aplenty, forgetting that my home is where I work long hours every day.

No, I am less a recluse than ever before. The remaining bright-dark wild places on the island help see to that. I now realize that the earth *is his*. We have all been set down in a place created for our growth—inward as well as outward. I now understand more clearly what Jesus meant when he reminded us that the Father knows when even a sparrow falls to the ground. I've blinked back tears when a little white-throated sparrow has lost its way in the often-blinding island light and crashed to its death against a window. If I care that much, how much must the Father care? About all of his earth.

Christmas on St. Simons Island is one of the most glorious times of the whole year. There are still a few colored leaves clinging to our deciduous trees in bright flags and the gray, waving banners of

Spanish moss never look cleaner or thicker than in winter when often they are a tree's only adornment. When it's possible for our families to spend Christmas with us, we're lyrical—we both dread every trip away—and, of course, we work for days decorating a carefully selected, enormous Scotch pine in our living-room bay. But each time we do, it seems almost superfluous, because we planted holly trees galore when we landscaped our property and until the gorgeous, gobbling cedar waxwings descend upon them (driving our favorite mockingbird out of his proprietary mind!) the heavy, bright red clumps of Palatka holly berries draped with silvery gray moss banners outdazzle all our efforts at tree decoration.

Sometimes it's chilly on Christmas day on the island—once there was even an exciting powdering of snow at the hearts of the palmettos —but even when it's been "cold" (40's) at Thanksgiving, we're often blessed with warm sun on the holy day itself. Mother and I have walked the beach on Christmas day in years gone by. Still, the mild weather, pleasant as it is after so many years in a northern city, is *not* what brings the special warmth to St. Simons Island at Christmas.

The remaining wild places alone do not bring it. Nor do the tall trees some of us are still fighting to keep free of the hideous screech of the chain saw.

The special St. Simons warmth comes, in my experience at least, *from the island people.* Our familiar and dear island friends—as varied an assortment as you'd find anywhere. One, who has been here about as long as we have, is a bookseller. The old-fashioned kind, who loves books. Another has a magnificent craft shop. Still another owns an authentic antique shop housed in one of our few remaining slave cabins. Another has just become well enough to leave our island rest home to return to her own apartment. She and her late husband rented us our first little beach cottage where we lived while our house was being built. Another—one of our dearest—is the island public stenographer, who not only gladdens our hearts daily just by *being,* but who skillfully types our manuscripts and helps with the never-ending mail. Another is the author of Georgia's *Land of the Golden Isles,* our most comprehensive local history volume.

Other friends, important ones, are our doctor, and the architect and the builder who made our home possible. Another is the cashier at the IGA supermarket where we've bought our groceries ever since we moved here. Two more are our nearest neighbors—at least half a mile away—but always close. They select a particularly beautiful orange from their tree for each of us every Christmas and leave it in our mailbox with a funny note.

A family who matter in particular are the Goulds, of St. Simons and Brunswick, and their relatives—all descendants of those about whom I wrote in the St. Simons trilogy of novels. And then there's Ida and Theo and Jean and Frances and the lady who cuts my hair. Three more are our librarians and another is the warm, lovely-voiced lady who takes my drugstore telephone orders and still another is the faithful gentleman who delivers them at night, along with our newspapers and fresh "yard eggs." And, more important to us than he guesses, is our beloved friend, who for more than five years has not only looked after our big yard and our house, but us too—in all the ways that count most. His wife is in the same place in our hearts, not only because she keeps our shirts and blouses spic and span, but because we know she loves us with the same kind of special love we have for her and her husband.

I'm sorry to report that the charming, quaint old Christmas custom—the first to shout "Christmas Gift!" must receive a gift—has almost died out. But the custom of love is still alive. And I'm at home in it, not only at Christmas, but every day. All my life I've been what my father used to call "a Christmas girl." Before I believed that God and sinners *were* reconciled that first Christmas, I loved the season and worked uncomplainingly at tree and gift trimming. But comparable only to that Christmas in 1949 when I *knew* for the first time that he *had* come to "love and save and free us" was my first Christmas on St. Simons Island.

Joyce had gone home to her parents that year, but I had just found St. Simons the month before and in my excitement, I picked up my mother in my home town and drove her down to the island to spend the blessed day in the pretty but drafty little beach cottage. I still lived in Chicago, but the die had been cast. I had found the island and I would never again be content away from it.

The research was just begun for the first novel, and one of the research "finds" we had made was a smiling, merry-eyed lady in her late eighties named Mrs. Lorah Plemmons. Lorah had been Anna Dodge's right hand in the Dodge Home for Boys just after the period covered by my novel, and it was from her that I learned not only what kind of great lady Anna Dodge had been long ago, but what a truly great lady could be today.

Lorah Plemmons, living alone in her little white house in the woods at Frederica, was out in her garage, "cleaning out a little," when Joyce and I drove unannounced into her large, flower-filled yard. A little bent, her silvery hair curling around the most welcoming face we'd ever seen, she came toward us across the yard. wiping the dust off her work-worn hands on a clean apron, smiling shyly. But the whole "Christmas thing" about that memorable moment was that with her bright "Yes, *come on in*, I'm Lorah Plemmons," I was suddenly at home forever on St. Simons Island.

Nine of our close ones—those we met soon after our arrival—lie in Christ Churchyard now. All younger than Lorah Plemmons, who celebrated her ninety-ninth year last summer. We know that if only from the weariness of the years she, too, could be with God by the time this is in print. But the gallant, great-hearted lady *has been* Christmas every day for us for all the years we've lived here.

That first Christmas, Mother and I, feeling a bit lonely, had driven up the island to Frederica to say Merry Christmas to Lorah and her twin daughters, Mary and Sarah—almost exactly my age, and teachers in New England, but, as always, home on St. Simons for Christmas. The Plemmonses saw us parking our car in Pretty Lane, hurriedly set two extra places at their Christmas table, and by the time we walked up to their door our welcome was so wide it might have been prepared for days.

Except for the past two years since my mother's broken leg episode (when I've flown home to her), we have spent Christmas with the Plemmonses in the now familiar inviting cottage which the daughters built with their own hands years ago. Even this year, when I'll miss it again, my thoughts, my heart, my island spirit will be there with them, under the big trees and the warm, loving smile of God. Lorah Plemmons, her blue eyes dancing, once said to me, "You know, Genie, one Christmas soon, I won't be here so you can look at me, but I'll *be here*. I'll be wherever you are, because the good Lord's not gonna change his mind. And he said we'd all always be together."

More than the loss of the big trees, the bright-berried cassina, the wild smilax and grapevines, we mourn the gradual loss of the small-town, provincial warmth possible where only a few people live and love and weep and have fun together. Our St. Simons post office is still a friendly place to go, but not quite the way it was when our beloved Mary Gould Everett was alive and its postmistress. The grocery store is still a happy, gossipy place, but it's a supermarket now, not small and intimate as in the old days. Jimmy Horne's Shrimp House on the mainland in Brunswick, where one could eat the freshest, most suc-culently cooked seafood on the east coast and where Christmas, Hallowe'en, Thanksgiving, Easter, Valentine's and St. Patrick's Day decorations were kept up all year long to save effort, has been torn down—Jimmy is dead—and new, box-like, stressed concrete structures will rise soon in what is being called "improving our waterfront." In many ways it will be an improvement, especially when one remembers the mud puddles in front of the ramshackle Shrimp House—and certainly I did not set out to write a nostalgia piece, a vacant cry for "the good old days." Of late, I find I don't feel in a crying mood at all. My perspective is leveling. I'm in a mood for giving thanks in a new way which I don't quite understand. Even four more golf courses (heaven forbid!) and the aching sight of still more acres of felled trees for paved parking lots and larger and still brighter shopping

centers and heavier traffic on Frederica Road—even Lorah Plemmons' homegoing some day—cannot and will not change the *every day Christmas feeling* of this island for me. *In the people,* I have found too much of God here, too much of a kind of quiet, caring love I'd somehow missed before.

There is no doubt that our quality of life is changing. If Frederica Road is four-laned, and there is talk of it, that will mean that the atmosphere of the once innocent island is gone forever. When we first moved here, no one ever locked his door. Now, Joyce and I— and Lorah Plemmons—have had to retain a security service. Still, this brings me to the simple point of all I've written: Another change has also taken place—a creative, redemptive change—and it took place in me. I was drawn to live here first of all because of the natural beauty and the history, but they did not change me. God uses people to bring about inner changes in his loved ones. The island people changed me. Changed us both. So, you see, all change is not for the worst. Certainly, it need not be. And the same continuing transformation can come to anyone, anywhere on the face of his earth, *if* by some means we have opened ourselves to the strong, eternal simplicity of giving love, welcoming love.

Outward change often frightens us, causes us to hug selfishly the memory of what we think of as "the good old days." The thought, even now, of the destruction of those breathtakingly beautiful trees that still arch over parts of Frederica Road tempts me to such selfish hugging. But what my "Christmas Island" has done for me is a far deeper thing. Invisible, except for the unforced smile which I now own. The unforced smile and the welcoming hand. I made myself smile in public for so long, even as a Christian, that I revel in this "Christmas every day" way of life. It is not "happiness every day." Christmas can and often does deepen grief. But all of life here to me now *is* ongoing, season in and season out. Islanders are not dependent upon "white Christmases" for the spirit of love, because we don't have snow once in five or ten years. I miss it now and then, but the inner climate of a Christian's heart does not have to depend upon the weather if the continuing change toward love is taking place. If growth has been irrevocably begun in us by the One who came on that first Christmas. Since there is no end to our growing season in this climate, I've even learned to begin the celebration of Easter at exactly the place it did begin—in a stable on Christmas day.

My island *has* changed. It will change still more, but what has happened to me here cannot change, because, as Lorah Plemmons said ". . . the good Lord's not gonna change his mind." And Christmas here, and where you are, began with Lorah's "good Lord."

Eugenia Price

31

WASN'T THAT A MIGHTY DAY

Wasn't that a mighty day
When Jesus Christ was born?
Star shone in the East,
Star shone in the East,
Star shone in the East,
When Jesus Christ was born!

Author Unknown

From THE SCHOLAR-GIPSY

And once, in winter, on the causeway chill
   Where home through flooded fields foot-travellers go,
   Have I not pass'd thee on the wooden bridge
Wrapt in thy cloak and battling with the snow,
   Thy face towards Hinksey and its wintry ridge?
     And thou hast climb'd the hill
And gain'd the white brow of the Cumnor range;
   Turn'd once to watch, while thick the snowflakes fall,
   The line of festal light in Christ Church hall—
Then sought thy straw in some sequester'd grange.

Matthew Arnold

A BLESSED CHRISTMAS

My days are so crowded
   and my hours are so few,
There's SO LITTLE TIME
   and SO MUCH TO DO . . .
My work is unfinished
   and my desk is piled high
And my unanswered mail
   seems to reach to the sky,
And the dear, thoughtful people
   whose unselfish praise
Has helped and inspired me
   in so many ways
I seem to neglect
   in the course of the year,
For while my intentions
   are deeply sincere,
It seems that my days
   are over and done
Before I have finished
   or halfway begun
All of the things
   I intended to do
And never find time
   to carry them through . . .
And so as another year
   draws to an end,
There are so many letters
   I didn't write or send,
And so many thanks
   that I never expressed
For the numberless ways
   in which I've been blest . . .
And this Christmas Greeting
   is my only way
To express once a year
   what my heart feels each day—
That I owe all I've done
   to the good Lord and YOU,

For I write with HIS help
  and your encouragement, too . . .
So thanks for your letters,
  your friendship and love,
And may God in His greatness
  look down from above
And grant you the things
  that mean most to you
And a real blessed Christmas
  and a glad New Year, too.
Helen Steiner Rice

THE ANSWER TO LIVING

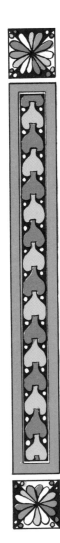
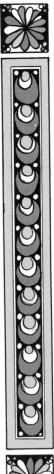

In this restless world of struggle
It is often hard to find
Answers to the questions
That disturb each troubled mind,
And our hearts are lost and lonely
As we search to find the key
To the meaning of all living
And to IMMORTALITY,
Little knowing we could find it
In the least expected places,
Never guessing we might see it
Written deep in human faces . . .
For the folks we meet in passing
Are all part of God above
And they truly are "our brothers"
HE commanded us to love . . .
For we who are so many
Are one body in the Lord,
And only when we learn to live
In agreement and accord
Can we hope to find the answer
That our troubled hearts are seeking,
For the answer to all living
God holds safely in His keeping . . .
And we who are a part of Him
Can only find it THERE
When we recognize HIS LIKENESS
In "OUR BROTHERS" everywhere!
Helen Steiner Rice

CHRISTMAS-GREETINGS

From a Fairy to a Child

Lady, dear, if Fairies may
    For a moment lay aside
Cunning tricks and elfish play,
    'Tis at happy Christmas-tide.

We have heard the children say—
    Gentle children, whom we love—
Long ago, on Christmas Day,
    Came a message from above.

Still, as Christmas-tide comes round,
    They remember it again—
Echo still the joyful sound
    "Peace on earth, good-will to men!"

Yet the hearts must childlike be
    Where such heavenly guests abide;
Unto children, in their glee,
    All the year is Christmas-tide!

Thus, forgetting tricks and play
    For a moment, Lady dear,
We would wish you, if we may
    Merry Christmas, glad New Year!
                    Lewis Carroll

EVERYWHERE, CHRISTMAS TONIGHT

Everywhere—everywhere, Christmas tonight!
Christmas in lands of the Fir tree and Pine,
Christmas in lands of the Palm tree and Vine,
Christmas where snow peaks stand solemn and white,
Christmas where cornfields lie sunny and bright,
Everywhere, everywhere, Christmas tonight!
                    Phillips Brooks

THE SNOW

It sifts from leaden sieves,
It powders all the wood,
It fills with alabaster wool
The wrinkles of the road.

It makes an even face
Of mountain and of plain—
Unbroken forehead from the east
Unto the east again.

It reaches to the fence,
It wraps it, rail by rail,
Till it is lost in fleeces;
It flings a crystal veil

On stump and stack and stem,—
The summer's empty room,
Acres of seams where harvest were,
Recordless, but for them.

It ruffles wrists of posts,
As ankles of a queen—
Then stills its artisans like ghosts,
Denying they have been.
                    Emily Dickinson

The Star

RISE UP, SHEPHERD, AND FOLLOW

There's a star in the East
On Christmas morn.
Rise up, shepherd, and follow!
It'll lead to the place
Where the Saviour's born.
Rise up, shepherd, and follow!
If you take good heed
To the angel's words and
Rise up, shepherd, and follow,
You'll forget your flocks,
You'll forget your herds.
Rise up, shepherd, and follow!
Leave your sheep, leave your lambs,
Rise up, shepherd, and follow!
Leave your ewes, leave your rams,
Rise up, shepherd, and follow!
Follow the Star of Bethlehem,
Rise up, shepherd, and follow!

Author Unknown

O Father, may that holy star
  Grow every year more bright,
And send its glorious beams afar
  To fill the world with light.
      William Cullen Bryant

SILENT NIGHT! HOLY NIGHT!

Silent night! holy night!
All is calm, all is bright;
Round yon virgin mother and Child,
Holy Infant so tender and mild;
Sleep in heavenly peace,
Sleep in heavenly peace.

Silent night! holy night!
Darkness flies, all is light;
Shepherds hear the angels sing:
"Alleluia! hail the King!
Christ the Saviour is born,
Christ the Saviour is born."

Silent night! holy night!
Guiding Star, lend thy light!
See the eastern wise men bring
Gifts and homage to our King!
Christ the Saviour is born,
Christ the Saviour is born.

Silent night! holy night!
Wondrous Star, lend thy light!
With the angels let us sing
Alleluia to our King!
Christ the Saviour is born,
Christ the Saviour is born.
      Joseph Mohr

THE FIRST NOWELL

From the Seventeenth Century

The first nowell the angel did say
Was to certain poor shepherds in fields as they lay;
In fields where they lay, keeping their sheep,
In a cold winter's night that was so deep.
   Nowell, nowell, nowell, nowell!
   Born is the King of Israel.

They lookèd up and saw a star,
Shining in the east, beyond them far,
And to the earth it gave great light,
And so it continued both day and night.

And by the light of that same star,
Three wise men came from country far;
To seek for a king was their intent,
And to follow the star wheresoever it went.

This star drew nigh to the north-west,
O'er Bethlehem it took its rest,
And there it did both stop and stay,
Right over the place where Jesus lay.

Then did they know assuredly
Within that house the King did lie;
One entered in then for to see,
And found the Babe in poverty.

Then entered in those wise men three,
Full reverently upon their knee,
And offered there, in His presence,
Their gold, and myrrh, and frankincense.

Between an ox-stall and an ass
This Child truly there born He was;
For want of clothing they did Him lay
All in the manger, among the hay.

Then let us all with one accord,
Sing praises to our Heavenly Lord,
That hath made Heaven and earth of naught,
And with His blood mankind hath bought.

If we in our time shall do well,
We shall be free from death and hell;
For God hath preparèd for us all
A resting-place in general.

THE THREE KINGS

Three Kings came riding from far away,
  Melchior and Gaspar and Baltasar;
Three Wise Men out of the East were they,
And they traveled by night and they slept by day,
  For their guide was a beautiful, wonderful star.

The star was so beautiful, large and clear,
  That all the other stars of the sky
Became a white mist in the atmosphere;
And by this they knew that the coming was near
  Of the Prince foretold in the prophecy.

Three caskets they bore on their saddle-bows,
  Three caskets of gold with golden keys;
Their robes were of crimson silk, with rows
Of bells and pomegranates and furbelows,
  Their turbans like blossoming almond-trees.

And so the Three Kings rode into the West,
  Through the dusk of night over hill and dell,
And sometimes they nodded with beard on breast,
And sometimes talked, as they paused to rest,
  With the people they met at some wayside well.

"Of the Child that is born," said Baltasar,
  "Good people, I pray you, tell us the news;
For we in the East have seen His star,
And have ridden fast, and have ridden far,
  To find and worship the King of the Jews."

And the people answered, "You ask in vain;
  We know of no king but Herod the Great!"
They thought the Wise Men were men insane,
As they spurred their horses across the plain
  Like riders in haste who cannot wait.

And when they came to Jerusalem,
  Herod the Great, who had heard this thing,
Sent for the Wise Men and questioned them;
And said, "Go down unto Bethlehem,
  And bring me tidings of this new king."

So they rode away, and the star stood still,
    The only one in the gray of morn;
Yes, it stopped, it stood still of its own free will,
Right over Bethlehem on the hill,
    The city of David where Christ was born.

And the Three Kings rode through the gate and the guard,
    Through the silent street, till their horses turned
And neighed as they entered the great inn-yard;
But the windows were closed, and the doors were barred,
    And only a light in the stable burned.

And cradled there in the scented hay,
    In the air made sweet by the breath of kine,
The little Child in the manger lay,
The Child that would be King one day
    Of a kingdom not human, but divine.

His mother, Mary of Nazareth,
    Sat watching beside his place of rest,
Watching the even flow of his breath,
For the joy of life and the terror of death
    Were mingled together in her breast.

They laid their offerings at his feet:
    The gold was their tribute to a King;
The frankincense, with its odor sweet,
Was for the Priest, the Paraclete;
    The myrrh for the body's burying.

And the mother wondered and bowed her head,
    And sat as still as a statue of stone;
Her heart was troubled yet comforted,
Remembering what the angel had said
    Of an endless reign and of David's throne.

Then the Kings rode out of the city gate,
    With a clatter of hoofs in proud array;
But they went not back to Herod the Great,
For they knew his malice and feared his hate,
    And returned to their homes by another way.
                    Henry Wadsworth Longfellow

The Story

My Dear Nephew:

A few days ago I was called in to prescribe for a sick man named Paul. He appeared to be a Roman citizen of Jewish parentage, well educated and of agreeable manners. I have been told that he was here in connection with a lawsuit, an appeal from one of our provincial courts, Caesarea or some such place in the eastern Mediterranean. He had been described to me as a "wild and violent" fellow who had been making speeches against the People and against the Law. I found him very intelligent and of great honesty.

A friend of mine who used to be with the army in Asia Minor tells me that he heard something about him in Ephesus, where he was preaching sermons about a strange new God. I asked my patient if this were true and whether he had told the people to rebel against the will of our beloved Emperor. Paul answered that the Kingdom of which he spoke was not of this world and he added many strange utterances which I did not understand, but which were probably due to his fever.

His personality made a great impression upon me and I was sorry to hear that he was killed on the Ostian Road a few days ago. Therefore I am writing this letter to you. When next you visit Jerusalem, I want you to find out something about my friend Paul and the strange Jewish prophet who seems to have been his teacher. Our slaves are getting much excited about this so-called Messiah, and a few of them, who openly talked of the new Kingdom (whatever that means), have been crucified. I would like to know the truth about all these rumors, and I am

Your devoted Uncle,
Aesculapius Cultellus, A.D. *62*

LONG, LONG AGO

Winds thro' the olive trees
  Softly did blow,
Round little Bethlehem
  Long, long ago.

Sheep on the hillside lay
  Whiter than snow;
Shepherds were watching them,
  Long, long ago.

Then from the happy sky,
  Angels bent low,
Singing their songs of joy,
  Long, long ago.

For in a manger bed,
  Cradled we know,
Christ came to Bethlehem,
  Long, long ago.

Author Unknown

TO REST WITH GOD

A STAR in the SKY,
  An ANGEL'S VOICE
Telling the world—
  REJOICE! REJOICE!
But that was centuries
  And centuries ago,
And we ask today
  WAS IT REALLY SO?

Was the Christ Child born
  In a manger bed
Without a pillow
  To rest HIS head?
Did HE walk on earth
  And live and die
And return to GOD
  To dwell on HIGH?

We were not there
  To hear or see,
But our hopes and dreams
  OF ETERNITY
Are centered around
  That holy story
When God sent us
  His SON in GLORY—
And life on earth
  Has not been the same,
Regardless of what
  The skeptics claim,
For no event
  Ever left behind
A transformation
  Of this kind . . .

So question and search
  And doubt, if you will,
But the STORY OF CHRISTMAS
  Is living still . . .
And though man may conquer
  The earth and the sea,
He cannot conquer
  ETERNITY . . .
And with all his TRIUMPH
  Man is but a clod
Until he comes
  To REST WITH GOD.

Helen Steiner Rice

THE V.I.P.*

'Twas late on the day before Christmas and all through the Mayfair Airport there was hustle, bustle, bedlam and happy confusion. A Very Important Person was due in on Flight 609, and anybody who was anybody in the town was there to greet him—the Governor, the Mayor, the Chamber of Commerce, et cetera, et cetera. Over the main entrance swung a huge white banner saying it for them: "Welcome, Henry Bascom, Mayfair's Own V.I.P." Henry was big in Washington, and he was coming home to spend the holidays with *them!* The red carpet was out for him. By five o'clock there wasn't even standing room.

The big plane spilled out its passengers into the lobby and they stood on tiptoe to see the big man. He should have been the first off the plane, but he wasn't. He wasn't even last. He wasn't there at all. The Governor figured that he must have missed the plane; the Mayor thought he may have sneaked away from the crowd in a limousine. There was muttering and murmuring and gnashing of teeth and a few yells of derision as the crowd milled about like so many lost sheep. They'd missed him!

No one noticed the man who skirted the mob and walked silently through a side door to the bus that would take him into town. He found a seat directly behind two jolly salesmen, each of whom knew by instinct of the road that the other was a salesman. One of them held out his hand and exulted, "Hi. I'm Ed Bingham. I'm in toys."

"Fred Williams. How's business?"

"O.K. Godfather games went big this year, and it wasn't bad in toy tanks and Frankenstein outfits, either. The kids love that stuff, bless 'em. After all, Christmas is for the kids, right?" (The man behind them started to say something, then thought better of it.) "What's your line, Fred?"

"I'm in guns. We sell the government—you know, rifles, 45's, machine guns, automatics, stuff like that. Had some real opposition, this year—the churches yelling about Vietnam and those whacky old women in sneakers screaming about peace, but we made out all right. Most sensible people know we've got to have guns if we want peace. They know it's nip and tuck between us and those godless Russians, and we're going to have to give them a licking, sooner or later. To my mind we'll never get peace till we kill off a million or so Communists."

The man behind them put his hands over his eyes and then over his ears, trying to shut out the sight and sound of Roman legions with bloody feet stomping across his land, bringing the Pax Romana—peace—and crosses.

They piled out of the bus right in front of the Mayfair Inn ("Your Home Away from Home"). He walked in and asked for a room. The desk clerk asked him, "Do you have a reservation?" No reservation. From behind the suddenly hard, professional face came words: "Afraid you're out of luck, sir. We're full up. Not a room in the place."

No room in the Inn. All right, he'd try elsewhere.

He tried four, five other inns, but the story was the same. No room, anywhere. Nothing. He went at last into Roger's Department Store ("The Friendly Store") just to get warm. He found himself no friends, but a madhouse. This was the last-minute crowd, making emergency purchases for someone who had everything, someone they had forgotten. They shoved. They pushed. They yelled. They fought and grabbed like so many crazed and starving peasants fighting for food. Loudspeakers overhead blared out a raucous, jazzed-up "Hark, the Herald Angels Sing." He heard a battle-weary clerk moan, "I hope to heaven I never see another Christmas." The angels stopped singing to make way for an announcement: "Closing time. Sorry, folks, closing time. Please leave the store now—and Merry Christmas." He found himself trapped in a swirling crowd that pushed him through the revolving doors, across the sidewalk and into the gutter.

He wandered now, not knowing where to go or what to do, through a labyrinth of closing doors and darkened shops. Through the windows of houses he could see the lights of Christmas trees, but these houses had locked doors, too. How long he wandered he never knew; it was long before he heard great bells ringing, and he traced the sound of them to the Cathedral.

Up and down the steps of the Cathedral moved men, women and children, happy either to get in or get out. He went in; an usher stopped him at a satin-covered chain stretched across the doorway and asked him, "Do you have a ticket?" No ticket. "Sorry, sir. Admission tonight is by ticket only."

He stared in unbelief and the usher, half in apology, explained, "I know it sounds funny, but we have to do it. Couldn't possibly let everybody in, so we take care of our own people first—you know, the people who support the Cathedral. Any seats left over after they're

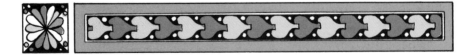

48

seated we give to the poor. If you'd like to take a chance and wait, please stand over there by that wall. . . ."

From where he stood with the usher, he could look all the way down the aisle to the altar. On the altar were vessels gleaming with silver and gold and set with precious stones. Around it moved many men clad in rich silks, and to one side sat one who seemed a king, sitting on a throne, with a crown and a shepherd's crook. He turned away; this was not for him. He paused only long enough to drop a small coin in a box marked "Money for the Poor."

Where now? He walked again—two blocks, six, eight, ten blocks—in a daze, fighting the depressing loneliness of the stranger alone in the heart of a great city. At last he stood clinging to an icy lamp post, murmuring into the darkness, "Father, forgive them."

A hand came out of the night and touched his arm; he turned to see a man in a dirty old overcoat, a cap in tatters, with rough, gnarled hands and kindly eyes. "Are you sick, sir? Can I help you?"

He could not even answer, and the man went on. "It isn't good to cry on Christmas Eve, sir. I know you are either ill or a stranger, and—please—if you have nowhere else to go, would you like to come home with me? We haven't very much. We're on relief—but we have enough for one more. Come and have supper with us."

Out beyond the bitter marketplace they walked, far out to a tumble-down, weather-beaten hovel at the ghetto's edge, where they were greeted by a smiling wife who seemed to be expecting him, a ten-year-old boy with the steel shackles of polio on his legs, and a very old grandmother either asleep or dying under the burden of her years.

He looked about him, at the room. The father said, "It used to be a stable, but we are very happy here." They sat around a battered table, gathered around a single flickering candle. The little cripple offered a child's grace:

> "Lord, we thank thee for this food,
> For home, and friends, and thou to bless;
> Help us to know and do what is good,
> And to remember those who have less."

For the first time in his little life, the boy prayed with his eyes wide

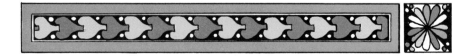

49

open, wistfully, in that ecstasy of childhood which sees that to which adult eyes are so often blind—as though he had known this stranger for a long, long time.

Then the stranger took the loaf of bread and broke it, and he drank with them from cracked and broken cups and ate of their poor, thin soup.

The grandmother touched no bread or soup; she sat as though she had been hypnotized. Her eyes, as she stared at him, were filled with the black ashes of a thousand broken, faded dreams, but in them was a sudden, trembling fire. It could have been the light of the candle that was giving glow to them—or it might have been the stranger.

When he left, he turned to face her and touched her cheek, and their eyes were locked in understanding. Then he vanished from their sight.

The old woman stood there like a statue, and then rushed out into the back yard. She looked down the road—but no, he was gone. Then she stood looking up at the silent, twinkling stars, and she heard the sound of music. All the hopes and fears of all her dead and difficult years rushed up in a torrent to her face and eyes, and she stretched the withered old arms and the claw-like hands above her head and screamed, "God! *Oh, God!*"

He found his way back to the airport—the only place, he reasoned, where he might rest awhile before he shook the dust of this city from his feet. The airport was empty now, except for two men taking down the welcoming banner for V.I.P. Henry Bascom. Said one to the other, "I just can't understand it. He must be in town, somewhere, but *we missed him.* Nobody, but nobody, saw him. Oh, well, come on. It's time to go home. Merry Christmas, Jake."

"Time for me, too, to go home," whispered the stranger to himself. Hardly anyone saw him leave—only the sleepy clerk at the ticket counter and a porter sweeping the floor and an old woman who looked out of a grimy window in a little shack far out of town. She watched the blinking lights of his plane grow dimmer and dimmer until they were lost in the folding arms of the night, and she could see only the stars.

Frank S. Mead

Shepherds at the grange,
  Where the Babe was born,
Sang with many a change,
  Christmas carols until morn.
Henry Wadsworth Longfellow

WHILE SHEPHERDS WATCH'D

While shepherds watch'd their flocks by night,
  All seated on the ground,
The angel of the Lord came down,
  And glory shone around.

"Fear not," said he (for mighty dread
  Had seized their troubled mind);
"Glad tidings of great joy I bring
  To you and all mankind.

"To you, in David's town, this day
  Is born of David's line
The Saviour who is Christ the Lord;
  And this shall be the sign:

"The heavenly Babe you there shall find
  To human view display'd,
All meanly wrapt in swathing bands,
  And in a manger laid."

Thus spake the Seraph; and forthwith
  Appear'd a shining throng
Of angels, praising God, and thus
  Address'd their joyful song:

"All glory be to God on high,
  And to the earth be peace;
Good-will henceforth from heaven to men
  Begin, and never cease!"

Nahum Tate

The Child

CHRIST IN THE CRADLE

Look, how He shakes for cold!
How pale His lips are grown!
Wherein His limbs to fold
Yet mantle has He none.
His pretty feet and hands
(Of late more pure and white
Than is the snow
That pains them so),
Have lost their colour quite.
His lips are blue
Where roses grew,
He's frozen everywhere:
All the heat He has
Joseph, alas!
Gives in a groan; or Mary in a tear.

Hon. Patrick Carey

54

THIS IS WHAT CHRISTMAS IS ALL ABOUT

CHRISTMAS to me is a GIFT from ABOVE—
    a GIFT of SALVATION born of GOD'S LOVE,
For far beyond what my mind comprehends
    my ETERNAL FUTURE completely depends
On that FIRST CHRISTMAS NIGHT centuries ago
    when GOD sent HIS SON to the earth below . . .
For if the CHRIST CHILD had not been born
    there would be no rejoicing on EASTER MORN,
For only because CHRIST was born and died
    and hung on a cross to be crucified
Can worldly sinners like you and me
    be fit to live in ETERNITY . . .
So CHRISTMAS is more than "GETTING and GIVING"—
    it's the why and the wherefore of infinite living,
It's the positive proof for doubting GOD never
    for in HIS KINGDOM life is forever . . .
And that is the reason that on CHRISTMAS DAY
    I can only kneel down and prayerfully say,
"Thank YOU, GOD, for sending YOUR SON
    so when my work on earth is done
I can look at last on YOUR HOLY FACE
    knowing YOU saved me alone by YOUR GRACE!"

Helen Steiner Rice

There are some of us . . . who think to ourselves, "If I had only been there! How quick I would have been to help the Baby. I would have washed His linen. How happy I would have been to go with the shepherds to see the Lord lying in the manger!" Yes, we would. We say that because we know how great Christ is, but if we had been there at that time, we would have done no better than the people of Bethlehem. . . . Why don't we do it now? We have Christ in our neighbor.

Martin Luther

It is good to be children sometimes, and never better than at Christmas, when its mighty Founder was a child Himself.

Charles Dickens

THE LAMB

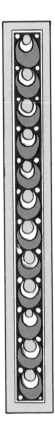

Little Lamb, who made thee?
Dost thou know who made thee?
Gave thee life, and bid thee feed
By the stream and o'er the mead;
Gave thee clothing of delight,
Softest clothing, woolly, bright;
Gave thee such a tender voice,
Making all the vales rejoice?
Little Lamb, who made thee?
Dost thou know who made thee?

Little Lamb, I'll tell thee,
Little Lamb, I'll tell thee:
He is called by thy name,
For He calls Himself a Lamb.
He is meek, and He is mild;
He became a little child.
I a child, and thou a lamb,
We are called by His name.
Little Lamb, God bless thee!
Little Lamb, God bless thee!

William Blake

THE FRIENDLY BEASTS

Jesus our brother, strong and good,
Was humbly born in a stable rude,
And the friendly beasts around Him stood,
Jesus our brother, strong and good.

"I," said the donkey, shaggy and brown,
"I carried His mother up hill and down,
I carried her safely to Bethlehem town;
I," said the donkey, shaggy and brown.

"I," said the cow, all white and red,
"I gave Him my manger for His bed,
I gave Him my hay to pillow His head,
I," said the cow, all white and red.

"I," said the sheep, with curly horn,
"I gave Him my wool for His blanket warm,
He wore my coat on Christmas morn;
I," said the sheep, with curly horn.

56

"I," said the dove, from the rafters high,
"Cooed Him to sleep, my mate and I,
  We cooed Him to sleep, my mate and I;
  I," said the dove, from the rafters high.

And every beast, by some good spell,
In the stable dark was glad to tell,
Of the gift he gave Immanuel,
The gift he gave Immanuel.

Author Unknown

THE STORKE

From the flyleaf of an Edward VI prayer book—1549

The Storke she rose on Christmas Eve
  And sayed unto her broode,
I now must fare to Bethlehem
  To viewe the Sonne of God.

She gave to eche his dole of mete,
  She stowed them fayrlie in,
And faire she flew and faste she flew,
  And came to Bethlehem.

Now where is He of David's line?
  She asked at House and Halle,
He is not here, they spake hardlye,
  But in the maungier stalle.

She found Hym in the maungier stalle
  With that most Holye Mayde;
The gentyle Storke shee wept to see
  The Lord so rudelye layde.

Then from her panntynge brest she plucked
  The fethers whyte and warm;
She strawed them in the maungier bed
  To keep the Lord from harm.

Now blessèd bee the gentyle Storke
  Forever more quothe hee,
For that she saw My sadde estate,
  And showèd Pytye.

Full welcom shall shee ever bee
  In hamlet and in halle,
And hight [called] henceforth the Blessèd Byrd
  And friend of babyes all.

HAPPY, HAPPY DAY! *

My friend Clements had married a beautiful and brilliant Polish girl —and it was her first Christmas in America. Some weeks before that day, she came to me with her eyes as big as saucers and said, "May I please asking of you the question?"

I said of course she could, and I hoped I'd know the answer.

"Is it," said Stasia, "that you celebrate on the same day the feast of St. Nicholas and the birth of the Christ?"

I said, "I—yes, I suppose we do. I never thought of it just that way. But, as a matter of fact, we do."

"But," said Stasia, sputtering as she does when she speaks English, "that is impossible! That it is not in any way possible that you should do it."

"No—" I said, "maybe it isn't. But—we try."

"I do not understand," said my little Polish friend. "On the day of St. Nicholas, that is the day of celebration of—of *things*. So we might say it. And of the family. On the day of St. Nicholas—before the day one goes forth into the forest nearby and cuts it down a nice tree. It is then to decorate with many bright colors—the red and the gold and the silver. And by the fireplace one is to hang up the stockings, so that when he comes down the chimney he will find them ready in which to put the presents. No?"

"Yes—" I said, "that is true."

"And on that day and the day after it, is to eat and drink, as much as it is possible for one to eat and drink, no?"

"Yes—" I said, "turkey and trimmings and eggnog—"

"To be sure," said Stasia, looking at me with very cold blue eyes. "And what," she said, "has this to do with the birth of the Christ in a poor manger to be the Savior of the world?"

"When you put it that way," I said, "I can see that it does not have anything to do with it at all. It's just—"

"Then," said Stasia, "why is it that you try to do it?"

"What do *you* do?" I said, remembering Rockne's conclusion that a good offense is sometimes the best defense.

"On the sixteenth of December," said Stasia, beginning to light up a little, "we celebrate the feast of St. Nicholas, the friend of the children. To do this, we string together the popcorn and the little red berries—how is it you call them? the cranberries—and we make ornaments of gold and silver, and the small cornucopias of all colors, and fill them with the small candies. And all these we hang on the pretty tree. Then we hang up on the mantel all the stockings of the small

ones of the family, and these are filled in the night by St. Nicholas—your Santa Claus—or it may be by his human assistants, the pappa and the mamma—no? Then we call all to the big dinner with the goose and the turkey and the pudding and the pie—and the wines and the fine brandy.

"We exchange then, too, the gifts for each other. Santa Claus, you will find, is the one who dispenses the gifts—but *not* on Christmas —either on the eve of St. Nicholas *or* on his own name day. *But* he is not to do this on the day of the Christ.

"Christmas—it is a *holy day*. It is to fast, to pray, to go to church at midnight and await the coming of our Lord. Of all days that are in the year, the most blessed and holy one is the day of Christ's birth. To me—and I must say it—from my country, it would be indeed the blasphemy to celebrate the birthday of Christ by eating too much and perhaps by drinking too much.

"It is not so in my country—nor the other countries in which I have been. I do not see how you do it."

I stood what my grandmother used to call *flabbergasted*.

To you it is necessary that I admit—you see, speaking of Stasia, *I'm* beginning to do it in Polish rhythm myself—I admit I had never thought about this odd, this *incredible*, mixture before in my whole life.

Christmas memories, of which—like you and everybody else in the world—I have many, began to crowd in upon me. *What* did I remember about *Christmas?* What did I remember best—out of which of Stasia's two different days, concepts, celebrations?

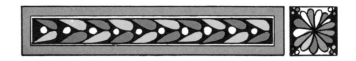

At my present age of *eighty*, I can look back—and forward—on Christmas as a child, as a teen-ager, as a mother, a grandmother, and now a *great*-grandmother. That's a lot of different viewpoints. And I stood very still trying to *let* the memories and their pictures and dialogues move by me, through me—a little bit in sequence, if possible.

No, no! This wasn't *possible!* I had been what was called a tomboy in those days, I could climb trees and hunt tarantulas, and ride a bronco as well as any boy—and even chop off the head of a rattlesnake or two. Impossible that I remember best that *doll* my Auntie Madge dressed for me the Christmas I was eight! The little blue sailor suit with the collar stitched in white, the party dress with the pink ribbon sash, above all the tiny, tiny patent leather Mary Janes. Bicycles—the twenty-two I got when I was ten—the saddle with the beaten silver trimmings—but not a *doll*. Even with a quilted bathrobe.

All right—so I remember the doll. Her name was Jo, after *Little Women.*

The Christmas my husband, Ike St. Johns, gave me a *bracelet*—I think that was the end of our fifteen years of marriage because I do not wear bracelets. I mean, it was the real end of a *hope* that I could make it work—or he could, for that matter.

It is on memories of Christmas, I find to my amazement, that my feelings about many people are founded. I had one friend, for instance, with whom I'd tried to keep up a pleasant relationship—until the Christmas that she sent me a fifteen-pound box of French chocolates. I don't eat chocolates, I'm not in favor of keeping huge boxes of confections around the living room for my grandchildren to gobble or, even worse, to get all over everything, including themselves. And there are always so many things that—that you can share, or pass around to others who need them. I—I never felt after that that we really spoke the same language. I don't really mind not speaking the *same* language, but there has to be some way we can understand each other.

And I have a very tender spot for my son, Richard, due to a Christmas episode. I knew he wanted a new bike, so I went down to a shop in Beverly Hills where they keep *all* kinds of bikes, and in a burst of the spirit of Christmas bought the most expensive one they had, a *racing* bike with brakes and a *horn* and everything. And I wheeled it under the Christmas tree and he received it with

cheers and thanks and rode around on it, and I felt just great. It wasn't until several weeks later that his sister, Elaine, told me he didn't want a *racing* bike. He wanted a sturdy, all-purpose one that —in fact—he'd hankered after for quite some time. I have always felt that was the kindest thing anyone could do—to put up with something he didn't want rather than spoil the pleasure in giving he'd seen on my face. It made me trust him very much.

It was the same way when once I looked up on Christmas morning and saw all my children really sparkling like candlelight as my son, Bill, said, "Look! Ma's got the most packages—isn't that super!"

All those are, I suppose, St. Nicholas Christmas memories. But are they? Or is the spirit of loving and giving—trying to make others happy—the most shining part of the birthday of Christ?

I thought about this for quite a while.

And then it came to me that once I'd seen the two combined in a way that made the tears come to my eyes.

My granddaughter Kris was seven—maybe eight—and she was learning to cook. (I teach all my grandchildren to play a good strong game of poker and to cook, and figure they'll get by.) She had baked a small round cake with white icing, and when I came down to dinner on Christmas Eve she was placing a large red candle right in the middle of it.

She gave me a big smile and said, "There! It just seems to me the Baby Jesus ought to have a birthday cake. Nobody ever seems to remember about that—so I made him one my own self."

And she stood there looking like one of the smaller angels herself, and she lit the candle and began to sing in a small sweet voice—

> "Happy birthday to you,
> Happy birthday to you,
> Happy birthday, dear Baby Jesus,
> Happy birthday to you."

So now every year we have a birthday cake—and all my grandchildren and *great*-grandchildren sing, "Happy birthday, dear Baby Jesus, happy birthday to you."

And I like that as well as anything to combine St. Nicholas Day, with its birthday candles and celebration, *and* the birth of our Lord.

But—let's all watch it, shall we?

Adela Rogers St. Johns

BRING A TORCH, JEANNETTE, ISABELLA

Bring a torch, Jeannette, Isabella!
Bring a torch, to the cradle run!
It is Jesus, good folk of the village;
Christ is born and Mary's calling:
Ah! ah! beautiful is the Mother;
Ah! ah! beautiful is her son!

It is wrong when the Child is sleeping,
It is wrong to talk so loud;
Silence, all, as you gather around,
Lest your noise should waken Jesus:
Hush! hush! see how fast He slumbers:
Hush! hush! see how fast He sleeps!

Softly to the little stable,
Softly for a moment come;
Look and see how charming is Jesus,
How He is white, His cheeks are rosy!
Hush! hush! see how the Child is sleeping;
Hush! hush! see how He smiles in dreams.

From the Old French

CRADLE HYMN

Away in a manger,
No crib for a bed,
The little Lord Jesus
Lay down his sweet head;
The stars in the heavens
Looked down where he lay,
The little Lord Jesus
Asleep in the hay.

The cattle are lowing,
The poor baby wakes,
But little Lord Jesus
No crying he makes.
I love thee, Lord Jesus,
Look down from the sky,
And stay by my cradle
Till morning is nigh.

Martin Luther

For unto us a child is born,
unto us a son is given:
and the government shall be upon his
    shoulder:
and his name shall be called
    Wonderful,
    Counsellor, The mighty God,
    The everlasting Father,
    The Prince of Peace.
            Isaiah 9:6, King James Version

THE ETERNAL LIGHT

Call him immortal, call him Truth and Light
    And splendor of prophetic majesty
Who bideth thus amid the powers of night,
    Clothed with the glory of divinity.

James Allen

THE LITTLEST ANGEL *

It happened this side of the Milky Way
When the littlest angel strayed to play
Tag with a bat. He then lost sight
Of the angel-flight that turned to the right
When they reached Cloud Nine and flew out of view.
He was lost and didn't know what to do.
He asked a night owl to show him the route,
But he didn't even give him a hoot!
His halo slipped sideways and caught on his ear
As he fingered a feather to wipe off a tear.

His wings were tired, and he wanted to rest,
So he circled around to find the best
Place he could land and stay for a while.
And there, just ahead, about a mile,
He saw a hillside dotted with sheep
Folded down on their knees and all asleep.
Setting his wings in an easy glide
He came in to light right beside
A newborn lamb that awoke with a bleat,
Shivering, tottering to his feet.

The littlest angel felt the chill
And covered the lamb with his wings until
The baby was warmed by the summery feathers
That sheltered him from the wintry weathers.
And now two little ones who were lost
Were found where heaven and earth had crossed.
The angel took the lamb to its mother,
Then looking upward he saw another
One of his kind, his very own,
Come to guide him home to the throne.

When the main flight of angels returned and sang
Till the courts resounded and echoed and rang
With the tale they told of Bethlehem's glory,
The littlest angel thought of his story:
Though he had seen neither wise men nor kings,
He had saved a small lamb under his wings—
But, since he was the youngest cherubim
It seemed unimportant—what happened to him.
Too tired to stay up, he fell into bed;
And a Hand placed his halo back on his head.

Ralph W. Seager

BETHLEHEM OF JUDEA

A little child,
    A shining star.
A stable rude,
    The door ajar.

Yet in that place,
    So crude, forlorn,
The Hope of all
    The world was born.

Author Unknown

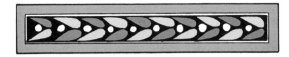

EX ORE INFANTIUM

Little Jesus, wast Thou shy
Once, and just so small as I?
And what did it feel like to be
Out of Heaven, and just like me?
Didst Thou sometimes think of *there,*
And ask where all the angels were?
I should think that I would cry
For my house all made of sky;
I would look about the air,
And wonder where my angels were;
And at waking 'twould distress me—
Not an angel there to dress me!

Hadst Thou ever any toys,
Like us little girls and boys?
And didst Thou play in Heaven with all
The angels, that were not too tall,
With stars for marbles? Did the things
Play *Can you see me?* through their wings?

Didst Thou kneel at night to pray,
And didst Thou join Thy hands, this way?
And did they tire sometimes, being young,
And make the prayer seem very long?
And dost Thou like it best, that we
Should join our hands to pray to Thee?
I used to think, before I knew,
The prayer not said, unless we do.
And did Thy Mother at the night
Kiss Thee, and fold the clothes in right?
And didst Thou feel quite good in bed,
Kissed, and sweet, and Thy prayers said?

Thou canst not have forgotten all
That it feels like to be small:
And Thou know'st I cannot pray
To Thee in my father's way—

When Thou wast so little, say,
Couldst Thou talk Thy Father's way?—
So, a little Child, come down
And hear a child's tongue like Thy own;
Take me by the hand and walk,
And listen to my baby-talk.
To Thy Father show my prayer
(He will look, Thou art so fair),
And say: "O Father, I, Thy Son,
Bring the prayer of a little one."

And He will smile, that children's tongue
Has not changed since Thou wast young!
Francis Thompson

THE VIRGIN MARY HAD A BABY BOY

The Virgin Mary had a baby boy,
The Virgin Mary had a baby boy,
The Virgin Mary had a baby boy,
And they said His name was Jesus.
He come from the glory,
He come from the glorious kingdom!
Oh, yes, believer!
He come from the glory,
He come from the glorious kingdom!
Author Unknown

WHAT YOU GONNA NAME
THAT PRETTY LITTLE BABY?

Oh, Mary, what you gonna name
That pretty little baby?
Glory, glory, glory
To the new born King!
Some will call Him one thing,
But I think I'll call Him Jesus.
Glory, glory, glory
To the new born King!
Some will call Him one thing,
But I think I'll say Emmanuel.
Glory, glory, glory
To the new born King!

Author Unknown

A CHILD'S SONG OF CHRISTMAS

My counterpane is soft as silk,
My blankets white as creamy milk.
   The hay was soft to Him, I know,
   Our little Lord of long ago.

Above the roofs the pigeons fly
In silver wheels across the sky.
   The stable-doves they cooed to them,
   Mary and Christ in Bethlehem.

Bright shines the sun across the drifts,
And bright upon my Christmas gifts.
   They brought Him incense, myrrh, and gold,
   Our little Lord who lived of old.

Oh, soft and clear our mother sings
Of Christmas joys and Christmas things.
   God's holy angels sang to them,
   Mary and Christ in Bethlehem.

Our hearts they hold all Christmas dear,
And earth seems sweet and heaven seems near,
   Oh, heaven was in His sight, I know,
   That little Child of long ago.

Marjorie L. C. Pickthall

BEFORE THE PALING OF THE STARS

Before the paling of the stars,
  Before the winter morn,
Before the earliest cockcrow,
  Jesus Christ was born:
Born in a stable,
  Cradled in a manger,
In the world His hands had made
  Born a stranger.

Priest and king lay fast asleep
  In Jerusalem,
Young and old lay fast asleep
  In crowded Bethlehem;
Saint and Angel, ox and ass,
  Kept a watch together
Before the Christmas daybreak
  In the winter weather.

Jesus on His mother's breast
  In the stable cold,
Spotless Lamb of God was He,
  Shepherd of the fold:
Let us kneel with Mary maid,
  With Joseph bent and hoary,
With Saint and Angel, ox and ass,
  To hail the King of Glory.

Christina G. Rossetti

The Celebration

A CHRISTMAS PRAYER

Loving Father, help us remember the birth of Jesus, that we may share in the song of the angels, the gladness of the shepherds, and the worship of the wise men.

Close the door of hate and open the door of love all over the world.

Let kindness come with every gift and good desires with every greeting.

Deliver us from evil by the blessing which Christ brings, and teach us to be merry with clear hearts.

May the Christmas morning make us happy to be Thy children, and the Christmas evening bring us to our beds with grateful thoughts, forgiving and forgiven, for Jesus' sake. Amen!

Robert Louis Stevenson

A CHRISTMAS HYMN

Love came down at Christmas,
Love all lovely, Love Divine;
Love was born at Christmas,
Star and Angels gave the sign.

Worship we the Godhead,
Love incarnate, Love Divine;
Worship we our Jesus:
But wherewith for sacred sign?

Love shall be our token,
Love be yours and love be mine,
Love to God and all men,
Love for plea and gift and sign.
Christina G. Rossetti

GO TELL IT ON THE MOUNTAIN

Go tell it on the mountain,
Over the hills and everywhere;
Go tell it on the mountain,
That Jesus Christ is born.

When I was a seeker,
I sought both night and day,
I asked the Lord to help me,
And He showed me the way.

He made me a watchman
Upon a city wall,
And if I am a Christian,
I am the least of all.

Go tell it on the mountain,
Over the hills and everywhere;
Go tell it on the mountain,
That Jesus Christ is born.
Author Unknown

THE CHRISTMAS FAMILY-PARTY

From *Sketches by Boz*

The Christmas family-party that we mean, is not a mere assemblage of relations, got up at a week or two's notice, originating this year, having no family precedent in the last, and not likely to be repeated in the next. It is an annual gathering of all the accessible members of the family, young or old, rich or poor; and all the children look forward to it, for two months beforehand, in a fever of anticipation. Formerly it was held at grandpapa's; but grandpapa getting old, and grandmamma getting old too, and rather infirm, they have given up housekeeping, and domesticated themselves with uncle George, so the party always takes place at uncle George's house, but grandmamma sends in most of the good things, and grandpapa always *will* toddle down, all the way to Newgate-market, to buy the turkey, which he engages a porter to bring home behind him in triumph, always insisting on the man's being rewarded with a glass of spirits, over and above his hire, to drink "a merry Christmas and a happy New Year" to aunt George. As to grandmamma, she is very secret and mysterious for two or three days beforehand, but not sufficiently so to prevent rumours getting afloat that she has purchased a beautiful new cap with pink ribbons for each of the servants, together with sundry books, and penknives, and pencil-cases, for the younger branches; to say nothing of divers secret additions to the order originally given by aunt George at the pastrycook's, such as another dozen of mince-pies for the dinner, and a large plum-cake for the children.

On Christmas-eve, grandmamma is always in excellent spirits, and, after employing all the children, during the day, in stoning the plums and all that, insists regularly every year on uncle George coming down into the kitchen, taking off his coat, and stirring the pudding for half an hour or so, which uncle George good-humouredly does, to the vociferous delight of the children and servants, and the evening concludes with a glorious game of blind-man's-buff, in an early stage of which grandpapa takes great care to be caught, in order that he may have an opportunity of displaying his dexterity.

On the following morning, the old couple, with as many of the children as the pew will hold, go to church in great state, leaving aunt George at home dusting decanters and filling castors, and uncle George carrying bottles into the dining-parlour, and calling for cork-screws, and getting into everybody's way.

When the church-party return to lunch, grandpapa produces a small sprig of mistletoe from his pocket, and tempts the boys to kiss their little cousins under it—a proceeding which affords both the boys and the old gentleman unlimited satisfaction, but which rather outrages grandmamma's ideas of decorum, until grandpapa says, that when he was just thirteen years and three months old, *he* kissed grandmamma under a mistletoe too, on which the children clap their hands and laugh very heartily, as do aunt George and uncle George; and grandmamma looks pleased, and says, with a benevolent smile, that grandpapa always was an impudent dog, on which the children laugh very heartily again, and grandpapa more heartily than any of them.

But all these diversions are nothing to the subsequent excitement when grandmamma in a high cap, and slate-coloured silk gown, and grandpapa with a beautifully plaited shirt-frill, and white necker-chief, seat themselves on one side of the drawing-room fire, with uncle George's children and little cousins innumerable, seated in the front, waiting the arrival of the anxiously expected visitors. Suddenly a hackney-coach is heard to stop, and uncle George, who has been look-ing out of the window, exclaims "Here's Jane!" on which the children rush to the door, and helter-skelter down stairs; and uncle Robert and aunt Jane, and the dear little baby, and the nurse, and the whole party, are ushered up stairs amidst tumultuous shouts of "Oh, my!" from the children, and frequently repeated warnings not to hurt baby from the nurse: and grandpapa takes the child, and grandmamma kisses her daughter, and the confusion of this first entry has scarcely subsided, when some other aunts and uncles with more cousins ar-rive, and the grown-up cousins flirt with each other, and so do the little cousins, too, for that matter, and nothing is to be heard but a confused din of talking, laughing, and merriment.

A hesitating double knock at the street-door, heard during a momentary pause in the conversation, excites a general inquiry of "Who's that?" and two or three children, who have been standing at the window, announce in a low voice, that it's "poor aunt Margaret." Upon which aunt George leaves the room to welcome the new comer and grandmamma draws herself up rather stiff and stately, for Mar-garet married a poor man without her consent, and poverty not being a sufficiently weighty punishment for her offence, has been discarded by her friends, and debarred the society of her dearest relatives. But Christmas has come round, and the unkind feelings that have strug-gled against better dispositions during the year, have melted away before its genial influence, like half-formed ice beneath the morning sun. It is not difficult in a moment of angry feeling for a parent to denounce a disobedient child; but to banish her at a period of general good-will and hilarity, from the hearth round which she has sat on so many anniversaries of the same day, expanding by slow degrees from infancy to girlhood, and then bursting, almost imperceptibly, into the high-spirited and beautiful woman, is widely different. The air of

73

conscious rectitude and cold forgiveness, which the old lady has assumed, sits ill upon her; and when the poor girl is led in by her sister, pale in looks and broken in spirit—not from poverty, for that she could bear, but from the consciousness of undeserved neglect, and unmerited unkindness—it is easy to see how much of it is assumed. A momentary pause succeeds; the girl breaks suddenly from her sister and throws herself, sobbing, on her mother's neck. The father steps hastily forward, and grasps her husband's hand. Friends crowd round to offer their hearty congratulations, and happiness and harmony again prevail.

As to the dinner, it's perfectly delightful—nothing goes wrong, and everybody is in the very best of spirits, and disposed to please and be pleased. Grandpapa relates a circumstantial account of the purchase of the turkey, with a slight digression relative to the purchase of previous turkeys, on former Christmas-days, which grandmamma corroborates in the minutest particular. Uncle George tells stories, and carves poultry, and takes wine, and jokes with the children at the side-table, and winks at the cousins that are making love, or being made love to, and exhilarates everybody with his good humour and hospitality; and when at last a stout servant staggers in with a gigantic pudding, with a sprig of holly in the top, there is such a laughing and shouting, and clapping of little chubby hands, and kicking up of fat dumpy legs, as can only be equalled by the applause with which the astonishing feat of pouring lighted brandy into mince-pies, is received by the younger visitors. Then the dessert!—and the wine!—and the fun! Such beautiful speeches, and *such* songs, from aunt Margaret's husband, who turns out to be such a nice man, and so attentive to grandmamma! Even grandpapa not only sings his annual song with unprecedented vigour, but on being honoured with an unanimous *encore*, according to annual custom, actually comes out with a new one which nobody but grandmamma ever heard before: and a young scape-grace of a cousin, who has been in some disgrace with the old people, for certain heinous sins of omission and commission—neglecting to call, and persisting in drinking Burton Ale— astonishes everybody into convulsions of laughter by volunteering the most extraordinary comic songs that were ever heard. And thus the evening passes, in a strain of rational good-will and cheerfulness, doing more to awaken the sympathies of every member of the party in behalf of his neighbour, and to perpetuate their good feeling during the ensuing year, than all the homilies that have ever been written, by all the divines that have ever lived.

Charles Dickens

A CHRISTMAS PRAYER

Oh Father up in heaven
We have wandered far away
From the Holy Little Christ Child
Who was born on Christmas Day . . .
And the Peace on Earth you promised
We have been unmindful of,
Not believing we could find it
In a simple thing called LOVE . . .
We've forgotten why You sent us
Jesus Christ, Your Only Son,
And in arrogance and ignorance
It's OUR WILL, not THINE, BE DONE . . .
Oh, forgive us, heavenly Father,
Teach us how to be more kind
So that we may judge all people
With our heart and not our mind . . .
And, Oh God, in Thy great goodness
May our guidance Christmas Night
Be the STAR the Wise Men followed—
Not a man-made satellite.

Helen Steiner Rice

CHRISTMAS AT SEA

The sheets were frozen hard, and they cut the naked hand;
The decks were like a slide, where a seaman scarce could stand,
The wind was a nor'-wester, blowing squally off the sea;
And the cliffs and spouting breakers were the only things a-lee.

They heard the surf a-roaring before the break of day;
But 'twas only with the peep of light we saw how ill we lay.
We tumbled every hand on deck instanter, with a shout,
And we gave her the maintops'l, and stood by to go about.

All day we tack'd and tack'd between the South Head and the North;
All day we haul'd the frozen sheets, and got no further forth;
All day as cold as charity, in bitter pain and dread,
For very life and nature we tack'd from head to head.

We gave the South a wider berth, for there the tide-race roar'd;
But every tack we made we brought the North Head close aboard;
So's we saw the cliffs and houses, and the breakers running high,
And the coastguard in his garden, with his glass against his eye.

The frost was on the village roofs as white as ocean foam;
The good red fires were burning bright in every 'longshore home;
The windows sparkled clear, and the chimneys volley'd out;
And I vow we sniff'd the victuals as the vessel went about.

The bells upon the church were rung with a right jovial cheer,
For it's just that I should tell you how (of all days in the year)
This day of our adversity was blessèd Christmas morn,
And the house above the coastguard's was the house where I
     was born.

O well I saw the pleasant room, the pleasant faces there,
My mother's silver spectacles, my father's silver hair;
And well I saw the firelight, like a flight of homely elves
Go dancing round the china-plates that stand upon the shelves.

And well I knew the talk they had, the talk that was of me,
Of the shadow on the household and the son that went to sea,
And O the wicked fool I seem'd, in every kind of way,
To be here and hauling frozen ropes on blessed Christmas Day.

They lit the high sea-light, and the dark began to fall.
"All hands to loose topgallant sails." I heard the captain call.
"By the Lord, she'll never stand it," our first mate Jackson cried
. . . "It's the one way or the other, Mr. Jackson," he replied.

She stagger'd to her bearings, but the sails were new and good,
And the ship smelt up to windward just as though she understood.
As the winter's day was ending, in the entry of the night,
We clear'd the weary headland, and pass'd below the light.

And they heaved a mighty breath, every soul on board but me,
As they saw her nose again pointing handsome out to sea;
But all that I could think of, in the darkness and the cold,
Was just that I was leaving home and my folks were growing old.

Robert Louis Stevenson

So remember while December
Brings the only Christmas day,
In the year let there be Christmas
In the things you do and say;
Wouldn't life be worth the living
Wouldn't dreams be coming true
If we kept the Christmas spirit
All the whole year through?

Anonymous

CHRISTMAS IN THE OLDEN TIME

On Christmas-eve the bells were rung;
The damsel donned her kirtle sheen;
The hall was dressed with holly green;
Forth to the wood did merry men go,
To gather in the mistletoe.
Thus opened wide the baron's hall
To vassal, tenant, serf and all;
Power laid his rod of rule aside
And ceremony doffed his pride.
The heir, with roses in his shoes,
That night might village partner choose;
The lord, underogating, share
The vulgar game of "Post and Pair."
All hailed, with uncontrolled delight,
And general voice, the happy night
That to the cottage, as the crown,
Brought tidings of salvation down.

The fire, with well-dried logs supplied,
Went roaring up the chimney wide;
The huge hall-table's oaken face,
Scrubbed till it shone, the day to grace,
Bore then upon its massive board
No mark to part the squire and lord.
Then was brought in the lusty brawn
By old blue-coated serving man;
Then the grim boar's head frowned on high,
Crested with bays and rosemary.
Well can the green-garbed ranger tell
How, when and where the monster fell;
What dogs before his death he tore,
And all the baitings of the boar.
The wassal round, in good brown bowls.
Garnished with ribbons, blithely trowls.
There the huge sirloin reeked: hard by
Plum-porridge stood, and Christmas pye;
Nor failed old Scotland to produce,
At such high-tide, her savory goose.

Then came the merry maskers in,
And carols roared with blithesome din.
If unmelodious was the song,
It was a hearty note, and strong;
Who lists may in their mumming see
Traces of ancient mystery;
White shirts supplied the masquerade,
And smutted cheeks the visors made;
But O, what maskers richly dight,
Can boast of bosoms half so light!
England was "merry England" when
Old Christmas brought his sports again;
'Twas Christmas broached the mightiest ale,
'Twas Christmas told the merriest tale;
A Christmas gambol oft would cheer
The poor man's heart through half the year.

Sir Walter Scott

HOW TO MAKE A TANSY

Take half a handful of Tansey, of the yongest ye can get, and a handful of young borage, Strawberry leaves, Lettice and Violet leaves, and wash them cleane, and beat them very small in a morter: then put to them eight Egges, whites and all, and six yolkes besides, and straine them together through a strainer & then season it with a good handful of sugar, and a Nutmeg beaten small. Then take a frying pan, and halfe a disk of sweet butter and melt it: then put your Egs to it, set it on the fire, and with a sawcer, or with a ladle, stir them till they be half baked: then put them into a Platter, and all, to beat them still till they be very small: then take your frying pan made cleane, and put a disk of sweet Butter in it, and melt it: then put your stuffe into your pan by a spooneful at once, and when the one side is fried, turn them and fry them together: then take them out, lay them in a platter, and scrape Sugar on them.

From A Booke of Cookerie, *1594*

Happy, happy Christmas, that can win us back to the delusions of our childish days, recall to the old man the pleasures of his youth, and transport the traveler back to his own fireside and quiet home!

Charles Dickens

79

OLD CHRISTMAS RETURNED

All you that to feasting and mirth are inclined,
Come here is good news for to pleasure your mind,
Old Christmas is come for to keep open house,
He scorns to be guilty of starving a mouse:
Then come, boys, and welcome for diet the chief,
Plum-pudding, goose, capon, minced pies, and roast beef.

The holly and ivy about the walls wind
And show that we ought to our neighbors be kind,
Inviting each other for pastime and sport,
And where we best fare, there we most do resort;
We fail not of victuals, and that of the chief,
Plum-pudding, goose, capon, minced pies, and roast beef.

All travellers, as they do pass on their way,
At gentlemen's halls are invited to stay,
Themselves to refresh, and their horses to rest,
Since that he must be Old Christmas's guest;
Nay, the poor shall not want, but have for relief,
Plum-pudding, goose, capon, minced pies, and roast beef.

Traditional

TO MAKE A DISH OF SNOW

Take a pottle of sweet thick Cream, and the white of eyght Egs, and beate them altogether, with a spoone, then put them into your cream with a dishfull of Rosewater, and a dishfull of Sugar withall, then take a sticke and make it clene, and then cut it in the end foursquare, and therewith beat all the aforesaid things together, and ever as it ariseth take it off, and put it in to a Cullender, this doone, take a platter and sette an Apple in the midst of it, stick a thicke bush of Rosemary in the Apple. Then cast your Snow upon the Rosemary and fill your platter therewith, and if you have wafers cast some withall, and so serve them forthe.

From A Booke of Cookerie, *1594*

THE THIEVES WHO COULDN'T HELP SNEEZING

Many years ago, when oak-trees now past their prime were about as large as elderly gentlemen's walking-sticks, there lived in Wessex a yeoman's son, whose name was Hubert. He was about fourteen years of age, and was as remarkable for his candor and lightness of heart as for his physical courage, of which, indeed, he was a little vain.

One cold Christmas Eve his father, having no other help at hand, sent him on an important errand to a small town several miles from his home. He travelled on horseback, and was detained by the business till a late hour of the evening. At last, however, it was completed; he returned to the inn, the horse was saddled, and he started on his way. His journey homeward lay through the Vale of Blackmore, a fertile but somewhat lonely district, with heavy clay roads and crooked lanes. In those days, too, a great part of it was thickly wooded.

It must have been about nine o'clock when, riding along amid the overhanging trees upon his stout-legged cob, Jerry, and singing a Christmas carol, to be in harmony with the season, Hubert fancied that he heard a noise among the boughs. This recalled to his mind that the spot he was traversing bore an evil name. Men had been waylaid there. He looked at Jerry, and wished he had been of any other color than light grey; for on this account the docile animal's form was visible even here in the dense shade. "What do I care?" he said aloud, after a few minutes of reflection. "Jerry's legs are too nimble to allow any highwayman to come near me."

"Ha! ha! indeed," was said in a deep voice, and the next moment a man darted from the thicket on his right hand, another man from the thicket on his left hand, and another from a tree-trunk a few yards ahead. Hubert's bridle was seized, he was pulled from his horse, and although he struck out with all his might, as a brave boy would naturally do, he was overpowered. His arms were tied behind him, his legs bound tightly together, and he was thrown into the ditch. The robbers, whose faces he could now dimly perceive to be artificially blackened, at once departed, leading off the horse.

As soon as Hubert had a little recovered himself, he found that by great exertion he was able to extricate his legs from the cord; but, in spite of every endeavor, his arms remained bound as fast as before. All, therefore, that he could do was to rise to his feet and proceed on his way with his arms behind him, and trust to chance for getting them unfastened. He knew that it would be impossible to reach home on foot that night, and in such a condition; but he walked on. Owing to the confusion which this attack caused in his brain, he lost his way, and would have been inclined to lie down and rest till morning among the dead leaves had he not known the danger of sleeping without wrappers in a frost so severe. So he wandered further onwards, his arms wrung and numbed by the cord which pinioned him, and his heart aching for the loss of poor Jerry, who had never been known to kick, or bite, or show a single vicious habit. He was not a little glad when he discerned through the trees a distant light. Towards this he made his way, and presently found himself in front of a large mansion with flanking wings, gables, and towers, the battlements and chimneys showing their shapes against the stars.

All was silent; but the door stood wide open, it being from this door that the light shone which had attracted him. On entering he found himself in a vast apartment arranged as a dining-hall, and brilliantly illuminated. The walls were covered with a great deal of dark wainscoting, formed into moulded panels, carvings, closet-doors, and the usual fittings of a house of that kind. But what drew his attention most was the large table in the midst of the hall, upon which was spread a sumptuous supper, as yet untouched. Chairs were placed around, and it appeared as if something had occurred to interrupt the meal just at the time when all were ready to begin.

Even had Hubert been so inclined, he could not have eaten in his helpless state, unless by dipping his mouth into the dishes, like a pig or cow. He wished first to obtain assistance; and was about to penetrate further into the house for that purpose when he heard hasty footsteps in the porch and the words, "Be quick!" uttered in the deep voice which had reached him when he was dragged from the horse. There was only just time for him to dart under the table before three men entered the dining-hall. Peeping from beneath the hanging edges of the tablecloth, he perceived that their faces, too, were blackened, which at once removed any remaining doubts he may have felt that these were the same thieves.

"Now, then," said the first—the man with the deep voice—"let us hide ourselves. They will all be back again in a minute. That was a good trick to get them out of the house—eh?"

"Yes. You well imitated the cries of a man in distress," said the second.

"Excellently," said the third.

"But they will soon find out that it was a false alarm. Come, where shall we hide? It must be some place we can stay in for two or three hours, till all are in bed and asleep. Ah! I have it. Come this way! I have learnt that the further closet is not opened once in a twelve-month; it will serve our purpose exactly."

The speaker advanced into a corridor which led from the hall. Creeping a little farther forward, Hubert could discern that the closet stood at the end, facing the dining-hall. The thieves entered it, and closed the door. Hardly breathing, Hubert glided forward, to learn a little more of their intention, if possible; and, coming close, he could hear the robbers whispering about the different rooms where the jewels, plate, and other valuables of the house were kept, which they plainly meant to steal.

They had not been long in hiding when a gay chattering of ladies and gentlemen was audible on the terrace without. Hubert felt that it would not do to be caught prowling about the house, unless he wished to be taken for a robber himself; and he slipped softly back to the hall, out at the door, and stood in a dark corner of the porch, where he could see everything without being himself seen. In a moment or two a whole troop of personages came gliding past him into the house. There were an elderly gentleman and lady, eight or nine

young ladies, as many young men, besides half-a-dozen men-servants and maids. The mansion had apparently been quite emptied of its occupants.

"Now, children and young people, we will resume our meal," said the old gentleman. "What the noise could have been I cannot understand. I never felt so certain in my life that there was a person being murdered outside my door."

Then the ladies began saying how frightened they had been, and how they had expected an adventure, and how it had ended in nothing after all.

"Wait a while," said Hubert to himself. "You'll have adventure enough by-and-by, ladies."

It appeared that the young men and women were married sons and daughters of the old couple, who had come that day to spend Christmas with their parents.

The door was then closed, Hubert being left outside in the porch. He thought this a proper moment for asking their assistance; and, since he was unable to knock with his hands, began boldly to kick the door.

"Hullo! What disturbance are you making here?" said a footman who opened it; and, seizing Hubert by the shoulder, he pulled him into the dining-hall. "Here's a strange boy I have found making a noise in the porch, Sir Simon."

Everybody turned.

"Bring him forward," said Sir Simon, the old gentleman before mentioned. "What were you doing there, my boy?"

"Why his arms are tied!" said one of the ladies.

"Poor fellow!" said another.

Hubert at once began to explain that he had been waylaid on his journey home, robbed of his horse, and mercilessly left in this condition by the thieves.

"Only to think of it!" exclaimed Sir Simon.

"That's a likely story," said one of the gentlemen-guests, incredulously.

"Doubtful, hey?" asked Sir Simon.

"Perhaps he's a robber himself," suggested a lady.

"There is a curiously wild wicked look about him, certainly, now that I examine him closely," said the old mother.

Hubert blushed with shame; and, instead of continuing his story, and relating that robbers were concealed in the house, he doggedly held his tongue, and half resolved to let them find out their danger for themselves.

"Well, untie him," said Sir Simon. "Come, since it is Christmas Eve, we'll treat him well. Here, my lad; sit down in that empty seat at the bottom of the table, and make as good a meal as you can. When you have had your fill we will listen to more particulars of your story."

The feast then proceeded; and Hubert, now at liberty, was not at all sorry to join in. The more they ate and drank the merrier did the company become; the wine flowed freely, the logs flared up the chimney, the ladies laughed at the gentlemen's stories; in short, all went as noisily and as happily as a Christmas gathering in old times possibly could do.

Hubert, in spite of his hurt feelings at their doubts of his honesty, could not help being warmed both in mind and in body by the good cheer, the scene, and the example of hilarity set by his neighbors. At last he laughed as heartily at their stories and repartees as the old Baronet, Sir Simon, himself. When the meal was almost over one of the sons, who had drunk a little too much wine, after the manner of men in that century, said to Hubert, "Well, my boy, how are you? Can you take a pinch of snuff?" He held out one of the snuff-boxes which were then becoming common among young and old throughout the country.

"Thank you," said Hubert, accepting a pinch.

"Tell the ladies who you are, what you are made of, and what you can do," the young man continued, slapping Hubert upon the shoulder.

"Certainly," said our hero, drawing himself up, and thinking it best to put a bold face on the matter. "I am a travelling magician."

"Indeed!"

"What shall we hear next?"

"Can you call up spirits from the vasty deep, young wizard?"

"I can conjure up a tempest in a cupboard," Hubert replied.

"Ha-ha!" said the old Baronet, pleasantly rubbing his hands. "We must see this performance. Girls, don't go away: here's something to be seen."

"Not dangerous, I hope?" said the old lady.

Hubert rose from the table. "Hand me your snuff-box, please," he said to the young man who had made free with him. "And now," he continued, "without the least noise, follow me. If any of you speak it will break the spell."

They promised obedience. He entered the corridor, and, taking off his shoes, went on tiptoe to the closet door, the guests advancing in a silent group at a little distance behind him. Hubert next placed a stool in front of the door, and, by standing upon it, was tall enough to reach to the top. He then, just as noiselessly, poured all the snuff from the box along the upper edge of the door, and, with a few short puffs of breath, blew the snuff through the chink into the interior of the closet. He held up his finger to the assembly, that they might be silent.

"Dear me, what's that?" said the old lady, after a minute or two had elapsed.

A suppressed sneeze had come from inside the closet.

Hubert held up his finger again.

"How very singular," whispered Sir Simon. "This is most interesting."

Hubert took advantage of the moment to gently slide the bolt of the closet door into its place. "More snuff," he said calmly.

"More snuff," said Sir Simon. Two or three gentlemen passed their boxes, and the contents were blown in at the top of the closet. Another sneeze, not quite so well suppressed as the first, was heard: then another, which seemed to say that it would not be suppressed under any circumstances whatever. At length there arose a perfect storm of sneezes.

"Excellent, excellent for one so young!" said Sir Simon. "I am much interested in this trick of throwing the voice—called, I believe, ventriloquism."

"More snuff," said Hubert.

"More snuff," said Sir Simon. Sir Simon's man brought a large jar of the best scented Scotch.

Hubert once more charged the upper chink of the closet, and blew the snuff into the interior, as before. Again he charged, and again, emptying the whole contents of the jar. The tumult of sneezes became really extraordinary to listen to—there was no cessation. It was like wind, rain, and sea battling in a hurricane.

"I believe there are men inside, and that it is no trick at all!" exclaimed Sir Simon, the truth flashing on him.

"There are," said Hubert. "They are come to rob the house; and they are the same who stole my horse."

The sneezes changed to spasmodic groans. One of the thieves, hearing Hubert's voice, cried, "Oh! mercy! mercy! let us out of this!"

"Where's my horse?" said Hubert.

"Tied to the tree in the hollow behind Short's Gibbet. Mercy! mercy! let us out, or we shall die of suffocation!"

All the Christmas guests now perceived that this was no longer sport, but serious earnest. Guns and cudgels were procured; all the men-servants were called in, and arranged in position outside the closet. At a signal Hubert withdrew the bolt, and stood on the defensive. But the three robbers, far from attacking them, were found crouching in the corner, gasping for breath. They made no resistance; and, being pinioned, were placed in an outhouse till the morning.

Hubert now gave the remainder of his story to the assembled company, and was profusely thanked for the services he had rendered. Sir Simon pressed him to stay over the night, and accept the use of the best bedroom the house afforded, which had been occupied by Queen Elizabeth and King Charles successively when on their visits to this part of the country. But Hubert declined, being anxious to find his horse Jerry, and to test the truth of the robbers' statements concerning him.

Several of the guests accompanied Hubert to the spot behind the gibbet, alluded to by the thieves as where Jerry was hidden. When they reached the knoll and looked over, behold! there the horse stood, uninjured, and quite unconcerned. At sight of Hubert he neighed joyfully; and nothing could exceed Hubert's gladness at finding him. He mounted, wished his friends "Goodnight!" and cantered off in the direction they pointed out as his nearest way, reaching home safely about four o'clock in the morning.

Thomas Hardy

NEW YEAR DINNER

Served on January 1, 1707, to thirteen guests of Squire
Timothy Burrell of Cuckfield, Sussex.

Plumm Pottage.   Plumm Pottage.
Calve's Head and Bacon.   Boil'd Beef, a clod.
Goose.   Two bak'd Puddings.
Pig.   Three Dishes of Minced Pyes.
Plumm Pottage.   Two Capons.
Roast Beef, sirloin.   Two Dishes of Tarts.
Veale, a sirloin.   Two Pullets.
Goose.

SING A SONG OF CHRISTMAS CAROLS *

Deck the Halls With Boughs of Holly . . . And wash the curtains and polish the silver. And clean out the fireplace and haul in the wood . . . And try to find the old tree base. And dig out those cartons of decorations to see how many are good for another year.

While Shepherds Watched Their Flocks by Night . . . Sit up late making doll clothes. And finishing a sweater and painting a sled. And helping your husband uncrate a bicycle . . . And then steal around checking on your own flock before collapsing into bed.

Good Christian Men, Rejoice . . . When the last box is finally wrapped and tied and in the mail, and you're at least halfway through addressing the greeting cards.

We Three Kings of Orient Are . . . Bearing gifts we traverse afar: To church and parties and school bazaars. And shut-ins and hospitals and children's homes. And that family whose mother is ill and whose father is out of a job.

O, Come, All Ye Faithful . . . Joyful and triumphant that somehow it's all done! The church bells are ringing, it's time to come . . . Come, children and neighbors and aunts and uncles and cousins— come and behold Him. O, come, let us adore Him!

Away in a Manger . . . No crib for a bed—a three-year-old is curled up in a pew, fast asleep.

It Came Upon the Midnight Clear . . . That little voice calling out: "Is it morning yet? Did Santa Claus come?"

Silent Night, Holy Night . . . All is calm, all is bright . . . at last . . . It is, it truly is . . . Sleep in heavenly peace.

Hark! the Herald Angels Sing . . . At the crack of dawn, "Get up, get up, Merry Christmas!"

Joy to the World . . . Let earth receive her king . . . And people their gifts, and parents their hugs . . . Let children run back and forth to each other's houses, and neighbors pop in for a cup of wassail and to admire the shining tree . . . Let heaven and nature and your own heart sing!

God Rest You Merry, Gentlemen . . . And women. Let nothing you dismay! Even though the whole house is an explosion of candy, nuts, papers, presents and ribbon; the tags are so mixed up nobody knows who to thank for what; and the cat is knocking the ornaments off the tree . . .

Add another log to the fire snapping so fragrant on the grate, baste the turkey already golden in the oven. Fling open the door to grandparents and other guests who come tramping up the snowy walk. With true love and brotherhood, each other now embrace.

God rest you merry, mothers and fathers and families and friends, at the end of this glorious Christmas day!

Marjorie Holmes

A CHRISTMAS CARMEN

Sound over all waters, reach out from all lands,
The chorus of voices, the clasping of hands;
Sing hymns that were sung by the stars of the morn,
Sing songs of the angels when Jesus was born!
   With glad jubilations
   Bring hope to the nations!
The dark night is ending and dawn has begun:
Rise, hope of the ages, arise like the sun,
   All speech flow to music, all hearts beat as one!

Sing the bridal of nations! with chorals of love
Sing out the war-vulture and sing in the dove,
Till the hearts of the peoples keep time in accord,
And the voice of the world is the voice of the Lord!
   Clasp hands of the nations
   In strong gratulations:
The dark night is ending and dawn has begun;
Rise, hope of the ages, arise like the sun,
   All speech flow to music, all hearts beat as one!

Blow, bugles of battle, the marches of peace;
East, west, north, and south let the long quarrel cease:
Sing the song of great joy that the angels began,
Sing of glory to God and of good-will to man!
   Hark! joining in chorus
   The heavens bend o'er us!
The dark night is ending and dawn has begun;
Rise, hope of the ages, arise like the sun,
   All speech flow to music, all hearts beat as one!

John Greenleaf Whittier

The universal joy of Christmas is certainly wonderful. We ring the bells when princes are born, or toll a mournful dirge when great men pass away. Nations have their red-letter days, their carnivals and festivals, but once in the year and only once, the whole world stands still to celebrate the advent of a birth. Only Jesus of Nazareth claims this world-wide, undying remembrance. You cannot take Christmas out of the calendar, nor out of the heart of the world.

Anonymous

THE PROMISE OF CHRISTMAS

Nothing I write the whole year through . . . Means more to me than this card to YOU . . . For you're more to me than a NAME and a FACE . . . More than SOME ONE I met SOME PLACE . . . You're one of Christ's messengers, sent to fulfill . . . His Christmas promise of PEACE and GOOD WILL . . . For only through folks I have met, like you . . . Can the PROMISE of CHRISTMAS ever come true . . . For the feeling of friendship that stirs the heart . . . To send Christmas greetings, is only the start . . . Of something deeper that's hidden inside . . . That we cover up with an "armor of pride" . . . But from time to time, it's bound to peek through . . . And I've glimpsed it often in folks like you . . . And that's why at Christmas I can never forego . . . Sending a message to all those I know . . . For somehow I feel YOU and I are a PART . . . Not just of "each other" but Christ's own heart . . . And He came at Christmas so we might find . . . That it's not enough to be *"casually kind"* . . . For life can only be PEACEFUL and GOOD . . . When we are *LOVED* and *UNDER-STOOD* . . . And there's only one way to understand . . . And that's to follow Christ's "new command" . . . "LOVE YE ONE ANOTHER AS I LOVED YOU" . . . Not just as friends and acquaintances do . . . For Christmas is more than a merry greeting . . . Christ gave it to us as a "SPIRITUAL MEETING" . . . So, blessed be the CHRISTMAS TIE that binds . . . The love in our hearts to the thoughts in our minds . . . And to those I've just met and to those I have known . . . MERRY CHRISTMAS, GOD BLESS YOU and MAKE YOU HIS OWN.

Helen Steiner Rice

THE FIR TREE

Out in the forest stood a pretty little Fir Tree. It had a good place; it could have sunlight, air there was in plenty, and all around grew many larger comrades—pines as well as firs. But the little Fir Tree wished ardently to become greater. It did not care for the warm sun and the fresh air; it took no notice of the peasant children, who went about talking together, when they had come out to look for strawberries and raspberries. Often they came with a whole potful, or had strung berries on a straw; then they would sit down by the little Fir Tree and say, "How pretty and small that one is!" and the Fir Tree did not like to hear that at all.

Next year he had grown a great joint, and the following year he was longer still, for in fir trees one can always tell by the number of rings they have how many years they have been growing.

"Oh, if I were only as great a tree as the others!" sighed the little Fir, "then I would spread my branches far around and look out from my crown into the wide world. The birds would then build nests in my boughs, and when the wind blew I could nod just as grandly as the others yonder."

He took no pleasure in the sunshine, in the birds, and in the red clouds that went sailing over him morning and evening.

When it was winter, the snow lay all around, white and sparkling, a hare would often come jumping along, and spring right over the little Fir Tree. Oh! this made him so angry. But two winters went by, and when the third came the little Tree had grown so tall that the hare was obliged to run around it.

"Oh! to grow, to grow, and become old; that's the only fine thing in the world," thought the Tree.

In the autumn woodcutters always came and felled a few of the largest trees; that was done this year too, and the little Fir Tree, that was now quite well grown, shuddered with fear, for the great stately trees fell to the ground with a crash, and their branches were cut off, so that the trees looked quite naked, long, and slender—they could hardly be recognized. But then they were laid upon wagons, and horses dragged them away out of the wood. Where were they going? What destiny awaited them?

In the spring when the Swallows and the Stork came, the Tree asked them, "Do you know where they were taken? Did you not meet them?"

The Swallows knew nothing about it, but the Stork looked thoughtful, nodded his head, and said:

"Yes, I think so. I met many new ships when I flew out of Egypt; on the ships were stately masts; I fancy these were the trees. They smelled like fir. I can assure you they're stately—very stately."

"Oh that I were only big enough to go over the sea! What kind of thing is this sea, and how does it look?"

"It would take too long to explain all that," said the Stork, and he went away.

"Rejoice in thy youth," said the Sunbeams; "rejoice in thy fresh growth, and in the young life that is within thee."

And the wind kissed the Tree, and the dew wept tears upon it; but the Fir Tree did not understand about that.

When Christmas time approached, quite young trees were felled, sometimes trees which were neither so old nor so large as this Fir Tree, that never rested, but always wanted to go away. These young trees, which were always the most beautiful, kept all their branches; they were put upon wagons, and the horses dragged them away out of the wood.

"Where are they all going?" asked the Fir Tree. "They are not greater than I—indeed, one of them was much smaller. Why do they keep all their branches? Whither are they taken?"

"We know that! We know that!" chirped the Sparrows. "Yonder in the town we looked in at the windows. We know where they go. Oh! they are dressed up in the greatest pomp and splendor that can be imagined. We have looked in at the windows, and have perceived that they are planted in the middle of a warm room, and adorned with the most beautiful things—gilt apples, honey cakes, playthings, and many hundreds of candles."

"And then?" asked the Fir Tree, and trembled through all its branches. "And then? What happens then?"

"Why, we have not seen anything more. But it is incomparable."

"Perhaps I may be destined to tread this glorious path one day!" cried the Fir Tree, rejoicingly. "That is even better than traveling across the sea. How painfully I long for it! If it were only Christmas now! Now I am great and grown up, like the rest who were led away last year. Oh, if I were only on the carriage! If I were only in the warm room, among all the pomp and splendor! And then? Yes, then something even better will come, something far more charming, or else why should they adorn me so? There must be something grander, something greater still to come; but what? Oh! I'm suffering. I'm longing! I don't know myself what is the matter with me!"

"Rejoice in us," said the Air and Sunshine. "Rejoice in thy fresh youth here in the woodland."

But the Fir Tree did not rejoice at all, but it grew and grew; winter and summer it stood there, green, dark green. The people who saw it said, "That's a handsome tree!" and at Christmas time it was felled before any of the others. The ax cut deep into its marrow, and the tree fell to the ground with a sigh; it felt a pain, a sensation of faintness, and could not think at all of happiness, for it was sad at parting from its home, from the place where it had grown up; it knew that it should never again see the dear old companions, the little bushes and flowers all around—perhaps not even the birds. The parting was not at all agreeable.

The Tree only came to itself when it was unloaded in a yard, with other trees, and heard a man say:

"This one is famous; we want only this one!"

Now two servants came in gay liveries, and carried the Fir Tree into a large, beautiful salon. All around the walls hung pictures, and by the great stove stood large Chinese vases with lions on the covers; there were rocking-chairs, silken sofas, great tables covered with picture-books, and toys worth a hundred times a hundred dollars, at least the children said so. And the Fir Tree was put into a great tub filled with sand; but no one could see that it was a tub, for it was hung round with green cloth, and stood on a large, many-colored carpet. Oh, how the Tree trembled! What was to happen now? The servants, and the young ladies also, decked it out. On one branch they hung little nets, cut out of colored paper; every net was filled with sweetmeats; golden apples and walnuts hung down, as if they grew there, and more than a hundred little candles, red, white, and blue, were fastened to the different boughs. Dolls that looked exactly like real people—the Tree had never seen such before—swung among the foliage, and high on the summit of the Tree was fixed a tinsel star. It was splendid, particularly splendid.

"This evening," said all, "this evening it will shine."

"Oh," thought the Tree, "that it were evening already! Oh, that the lights may soon be lit up! When may that be done? Will the sparrows fly against the panes? Shall I grow fast here, and stand adorned in summer and winter?"

Yes, he did not guess badly. But he had a complete backache from mere longing, and backache is just as bad for a tree as a headache for a person.

At last the candles were lighted. What a brilliance, what a splendor! The Tree trembled so in all its branches that one of the candles set fire to a green twig, and it was scorched.

"Heaven preserve us!" cried the young ladies; and they hastily put the fire out.

Now the Tree might not even tremble. Oh, that was terrible! It was so afraid of setting fire to some of its ornaments, and it was quite bewildered with all the brilliance. And now the folding doors were thrown wide open, and a number of children rushed in as if they would have overturned the whole Tree; the older people followed more deliberately. The little ones stood quite silent, but only for a minute; then they shouted till the room rang; they danced gleefully round the Tree, and one present after another was plucked from it.

"What are they about?" thought the Tree. "What's going to be done?"

And the candles burned down to the twigs, and as they burned down they were extinguished, and then the children received permission to plunder the Tree. Oh! they rushed in upon it, so that every branch cracked again; if it had not been fastened by the top and by the golden star to the ceiling, it would have fallen down.

The children danced about with their pretty toys. No one looked at the Tree except one old man, who came up and peeped among the branches, but only to see if a fig or an apple had not been forgotten.

"A story! A story!" shouted the children; and they drew a little fat man toward the Tree; and he sat down just beneath it—"for then we shall be in the green wood," said he, "and the tree may have the advantage of listening to my tale. But I can only tell one. Will you hear the story of Ivede-Avede, or of Klumpey-Dumpey, who fell downstairs,

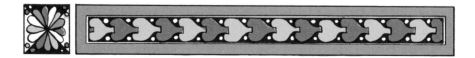

96

and still was raised up to honor and married the Princess?"

"Ivede-Avede!" cried some, "Klumpey-Dumpey!" cried others, and there was a great crying and shouting. Only the Fir Tree was quite silent, and thought, "Shall I not be in it? Shall I have nothing to do in it?" But he had been in the evening's amusement, and had done what was required of him.

And the fat man told about Klumpey-Dumpey who fell downstairs and yet was raised to honor and married a Princess. And the children clapped their hands and cried, "Tell another! tell another!" and they wanted to hear about Ivede-Avede; but they only got the story of Klumpey-Dumpey. The Fir Tree stood quite silent and thoughtful; never had the birds in the wood told such a story as that. Klumpey-Dumpey fell downstairs, and yet came to honor and married a Princess!

"Yes, so it happens in the world!" thought the Fir Tree, and believed it must be true, because that was such a nice man who told it.

"Well, who can know? Perhaps I shall fall downstairs, too, and marry a Princess!" And it looked forward with pleasure to being adorned again, the next evening, with candles and toys, gold and fruit. "Tomorrow I shall not tremble," it thought.

"I shall rejoice in all my splendor. Tomorrow I shall hear the story of Klumpey-Dumpey again, and perhaps that of Ivede-Avede, too."

And the Tree stood all night quiet and thoughtful.

In the morning the servants and the chambermaid came in.

"Now my splendor will begin afresh," thought the Tree. But they dragged him out of the room, and upstairs to the garret, and here they put him in a dark corner where no daylight shone.

"What's the meaning of this?" thought the Tree. "What am I to do here? What is to happen?"

And he leaned against the wall, and thought, and thought. And he had time enough, for days and nights went by, and nobody came up; and when at length some one came, it was only to put some great boxes in a corner. Now the Tree stood quite hidden away, and the supposition is that it was quite forgotten.

"Now it's winter outside," thought the Tree. "The earth is hard and covered with snow, and people cannot plant me; therefore I suppose I'm to be sheltered here until Spring comes. How considerate that is! How good people are! If it were only not so dark here, and so terribly solitary!—not even a little hare? That was pretty out there in the wood,

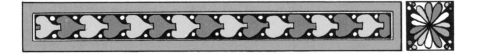

when the snow lay thick and the hare sprang past; yes, even when he jumped over me; but then I did not like it. It is terribly lonely up here!"

"Piep! piep!" said a little Mouse, and crept forward, and then came another little one. They smelled at the Fir Tree, and then slipped among the branches.

"It's horribly cold," said the two little Mice, "or else it would be comfortable here. Don't you think so, old Fir Tree?"

"I'm not old at all," said the Fir Tree. "There are many much older than I."

"Where do you come from?" asked the Mice. "And what do you know?" They were dreadfully inquisitive. "Tell us about the most beautiful spot on earth. Have you been there? Have you been in the storeroom, where cheeses lie on the shelves, and hams hang from the ceiling, where one dances on tallow candles, and goes in thin and comes out fat?"

"I don't know that," replied the Tree; "but I know the wood, where the sun shines and the birds sing."

And then it told all about its youth.

And the little Mice had never heard anything of the kind; and they listened and said:

"What a number of things you have seen! How happy you must have been!"

"I?" replied the Fir Tree; and it thought about what it had told. "Yes, those were really quite happy times." But then he told of the Christmas Day, when he had been hung with sweetmeats and candles.

"Oh!" said the little Mice, "how happy you have been, you old Fir Tree!"

"I'm not old at all," said the Tree. "I only came out of the wood this winter. I'm only rather backward in my growth."

"What splendid stories you can tell!" said the little Mice.

And the next night they came with four other little Mice, to hear what the Tree had to relate; and the more it said, the more clearly did it remember everything, and thought. "Those were quite merry days! But they may come again. Klumpey-Dumpey fell downstairs, and yet he married a Princess. Perhaps I shall marry a Princess, too!" And the Fir Tree thought of a pretty little Birch Tree that grew out in the forest; for the Fir Tree, that Birch was a real Princess.

"Who's Klumpey-Dumpey?" asked the little Mice.

And then the Fir Tree told the whole story. It could remember every single word; and the little Mice were ready to leap to the very top of the Tree with pleasure. Next night a great many more Mice came, and on Sunday two Rats even appeared; but these thought the story was not pretty, and the little Mice were sorry for that, for now they also did not like it so much as before.

"Do you know only one story?" asked the Rats.

"Only that one," replied the Tree. "I heard that on the happiest evening of my life; I did not think then how happy I was."

"That's a very miserable story. Don't you know any about bacon and tallow candles—a storeroom story?"

"No," said the Tree.

"Then we'd rather not hear you," said the Rats.

And they went back to their own people. The little Mice at last stayed away also; and then the Tree sighed and said:

"It was very nice when they sat round me, the merry little Mice, and listened when I spoke to them. Now that's past too. But I shall remember to be pleased when they take me out."

But when did that happen? Why, it was one morning that people came and rummaged in the garret; the boxes were put away, and the Tree brought out; they certainly threw him rather roughly on the floor, but a servant dragged him away at once to the stairs, where the day-light shone.

"Now life is beginning again!" thought the Tree.

It felt the fresh air and the first sunbeam, and now it was out in the courtyard. Everything passed so quickly that the Tree quite forgot to look at itself, there was so much to look at all round. The court-yard was close to a garden, and here everything was blooming; the roses hung fresh over the paling, the linden trees were in blossom, and the swallows cried, "Quinze-wit! quinze-wit! my husband's come!" But it was not the Fir Tree they meant.

"Now I shall live!" said the Tree, rejoicingly, and spread its branches far out; but, alas! they were all withered and yellow; and it lay in the corner among nettles and weeds. The tinsel star was still upon it, and shone in the bright sunshine.

In the courtyard a couple of the merry children were playing who had danced round the Tree at Christmas time, and had rejoiced over it. One of the youngest ran up and tore off the golden star.

"Look what is sticking to the ugly old fir tree!" said the child, and he trod upon the branches till they cracked again under his boots.

And the Tree looked at all the blooming flowers and the splendor of the garden, and then looked at itself, and wished it had remained in the dark corner of the garret; it thought of its fresh youth in the wood, of the merry Christmas Eve, and of the little Mice which had listened so pleasantly to the story of Klumpey-Dumpey.

"Past! past!" said the old Tree. "Had I but rejoiced when I could have done so! Past! past!"

And the servant came and chopped the Tree into little pieces; a whole bundle lay there; it blazed brightly under the great brewing copper, and it sighed deeply, and each sigh was like a little shot; and the children who were at play there ran up and seated themselves at the fire, looked into it, and cried "Puff! puff!" But at each explosion, which was a deep sigh, the Tree thought of a summer day in the woods, or of a winter night there, when the stars beamed; he thought of Christmas Eve and of Klumpey-Dumpey, the only story he had ever heard or knew how to tell; and then the Tree was burned.

The boys played in the garden, and the youngest had on his breast a golden star, which the Tree had worn on its happiest evening. Now that was past, and the Tree's life was past, and the story is past too: past! past!—and that's the way with all stories.

Hans Christian Andersen

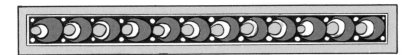

THE LEGEND OF THE CHRISTMAS TREE

Most children have seen a Christmas tree, and many know that the pretty and pleasant custom of hanging gifts on its boughs comes from Germany; but perhaps few have heard or read the story that is told to little German children, respecting the origin of this custom. The story is called "The Little Stranger," and runs thus:

In a small cottage on the borders of a forest lived a poor laborer, who gained a scanty living by cutting wood. He had a wife and two children who helped him in his work. The boy's name was Valentine, and the girl was called Mary. They were obedient, good children, and a great comfort to their parents. One winter evening, this happy little family were sitting quietly around the hearth, the snow and the wind raging outside, while they ate their supper of dry bread, when a gentle tap was heard on the window, and a childish voice cried from without; "Oh, let me in, pray! I am a poor child, with nothing to eat, and no home to go to, and I shall die of cold and hunger unless you let me in."

Valentine and Mary jumped up from the table and ran to open the door, saying: "Come in, poor little child! We have not much to give you, but whatever we have we will share with you."

The stranger-child came in and warmed his frozen hands and feet at the fire, and the children gave him the best they had to eat, saying: "You must be tired, too, poor child! Lie down on our bed; we can sleep on the bench for one night."

Then said the little stranger-child: "Thank God for all your kindness to me!"

So they took their little guest into their sleeping-room, laid him on the bed, covered him over, and said to each other: "How thankful we ought to be! We have warm rooms and a cozy bed, while this poor child has only heaven for his roof and the cold earth for his sleeping-place."

When their father and mother went to bed, Mary and Valentine lay quite contentedly on the bench near the fire, saying, before they fell asleep: "The stranger-child will be so happy to-night in his warm bed!"

These kind children had not slept many hours before Mary awoke, and softly whispered to her brother: "Valentine, dear, wake, and listen to the sweet music under the window."

Then Valentine rubbed his eyes and listened. It was sweet music indeed, and sounded like beautiful voices singing to the tones of a harp:

> "Oh holy Child, we greet thee! bringing
> Sweet strains of harp to aid our singing.
> "Thou, holy Child, in peace art sleeping,
> While we our watch without are keeping.
> "Blest be the house wherein thou liest,
> Happiest on earth, to heaven the nighest."

The children listened, while a solemn joy filled their hearts; then they stepped softly to the window to see who might be without.

In the east was a streak of rosy dawn, and in its light they saw a group of children standing before the house, clothed in silver garments, holding golden harps in their hands. Amazed at this sight, the children were still gazing out of the window, when a light tap caused them to turn around. There stood the stranger-child before them clad in a golden dress, with a gleaming radiance round his curling hair. "I am the little Christ-child," he said, "who wanders through the world bringing peace and happiness to good children. You took me in and cared for me when you thought me a poor child, and now you shall have my blessing for what you have done."

A fir tree grew near the house; and from this he broke a twig, which he planted in the ground, saying: "This twig shall become a tree, and shall bring forth fruit year by year for you."

No sooner had he done this than he vanished, and with him the little choir of angels. But the fir-branch grew and became a Christmas tree, and on its branches hung golden apples and silver nuts every Christmas-tide.

Such is the story told to German children concerning their beautiful Christmas trees, though we know that the real little Christ-child can never be wandering, cold and homeless, again in our world, inasmuch as he is safe in heaven by his Father's side; yet we may gather from this story the same truth which the Bible plainly tells us— that anyone who helps a Christian child in distress, it will be counted unto him as if he had indeed done it unto Christ himself. "Inasmuch as ye have done it unto the least of these, my brethren, ye have done it unto me."

Clement Clarke Moore

The Giving

GIOVANNI'S GIFTS

There is nothing I can give you
which you have not; but there is much, very much
that, while I cannot give it, you can take.

No heaven can come to us unless our hearts
find rest in today. Take heaven!
No peace lies in the future which is not hidden
in the present. Take peace!

The gloom of the world is but a shadow.
Behind it, yet within our reach, is joy. Take joy!
There is radiance and glory in the darkness
could we but see, and to see, we have only to look.
I beseech you to look.

Life is so generous a giver, but we,
judging its gifts by the covering,
cast them away as ugly, or heavy, or hard.
Know the covering, and you will find beneath it,
a living splendor, woven of love, by wisdom,
with power.

Welcome it, grasp it, and you touch the
angel's hand that brings it to you.
Everything we call a trial, a sorrow, or a duty,
believe me, that angel's hand is there: the
          gift is there,
and the wonder of an overshadowing presence.
Our joys, too; be not content with them as joys.
They, too, conceal diviner gifts.

Life is so full of meaning and purpose,
so full of beauty—beneath its covering—
that you will find earth but cloaks your heaven.

Courage then to claim it; that is all!
But courage you have; and the knowledge that we
are pilgrims together,
wending through unknown country, home.

And so, at this Christmas time, I greet you.
Not quite as the world sends greetings,
but with profound esteem and with the prayer
that for you, now and forever,
the day breaks and the shadows flee away.

Fra Giovanni

Selfishness makes Christmas a burden: love makes it a delight.

Anonymous

WHAT CHILDREN TEACH US ABOUT CHRISTMAS

The Christmas my son was twelve, he made most of the gifts he gave. There were sea shells gathered during the summer on the Cape Cod beaches, which Peter painted and shellacked as ashtrays for assorted male relatives. For an aunt there was a decorated cookie jar made from an old earthenware crock. A birdhouse which he made for his grandmother had a picket fence, a red chimney, a television antenna, and rambler roses (or was it wisteria?) painted over the door. I am not sure that the birds appreciated all these embellishments, but the grandmother definitely did. The *pièce de resistance* that Christmas was a toy chest. Peter's grandfather helped him to build it. When completed, the chest even had casters and rope handles. Then I helped with the sketching in of decorations. On a pale pink background was Nanny Etticoat in a White Petticoat; the Big, Big Coo; Wynken, Blynken and Nod; sundry fairies and elves. Inside the cover was a fairy castle complete with turrets, drawbridge and moat.

The small cousin for whom this chest was made adored it and has used it ever since. Peter loved making it. Christmas Morning saw him almost bursting with pride when he rolled the toy chest in to place it under the family tree and heard the expressions of admiration over his handiwork.

I doubt that Peter now remembers what I gave him that same Christmas. It was an English bicycle which he very much wanted. The bicycle has long since been broken; the toy chest, the birdhouse and the cookie jar are still in use, still family conversation pieces. There is no question that one twelve-year-old received far more pleasure out of what he gave than what he received that Christmas. He learned for himself that it actually is more blessed (and "blessed" really means "happy") to give than to receive.

This law of life was true for one boy, as it is for any of us, only because the boy gave of himself—many hours of his time, of loving thought, of work with his hands—along with the gifts.

I made this same discovery myself at a slightly earlier age than my son. The year that I was eleven, I started Christmas preparations quite early in September. As the gifts were completed, I piled them up on two closet shelves cleared for that purpose. There were small rustic Yule logs with fat red candles, meant for mantel and table decorations; trays with imprisoned and preserved butterflies on milkweed and pressed wild-flower backgrounds; pillowcases I had embroidered; tea towels I had hemmed; crepe-paper dolls with bouffant skirts supposed to hide powder boxes on dressing tables. It was the only year I did it.

How much my relatives appreciated these gifts I do not know. But the effort provided me with an inner satisfaction which I've never forgotten. The proof is that this one Christmas stands out glowingly above every other Christmas of my growing-up years.

In analyzing, however, what children can teach us about the fun of giving oneself along with the gifts, I dare not be oversentimental or unrealistic about children—my own or anyone else's. My own son, who seems to be about average, came with built-in egocentricity. The Christmas want-lists of my child, as of many, are sometimes yards long. Doting relatives and department-store Santas with their "And now tell old Santa what *you* want for Christmas, little boy" act like emotional Vigoro to help this me-first complex to flourish.

But living with self at the center never brings happiness to either child or adult. The law of diminishing return soon sets in. In every human being from three to ninety-three, selfishness wars with something deeper—also built in. That something is the instinctive need for fellowship, for a feeling of closeness with other human beings. The poet John Donne was right when he said, "No man is an island . . ."

The feeling of closeness to other people, of the togetherness of all human beings, flourishes at Christmastime. During this one brief season each year, our frustrated old world almost achieves the Kingdom of God on earth. For the term "Kingdom of God" really means "kingdom of right relationships," and this is specifically what the Christ child came to earth to make possible.

The spirit that finds it all but impossible to hold a grudge, a spirit of friendliness and love born out of sheer good will—this is the Kingdom of God on earth. Even during the Yuletide season, grownups step into that kingdom a little warily, somewhat self-consciously, whereas children take to it naturally and joyously. In doing so, they prove to the most cynical of us that the Kingdom of Heaven on earth —the "good will toward men" of which the first Christmas angels sang—is no fantasy. Its achievement is altogether possible. This spirit *could* come to earth, not just at Christmas but all year, if only we'd let it.

A child whom I know well, when about three, had one favorite story, "Tell me about Christmas, Mummy," she would plead. It might be steaming midsummer in the nation's capital, the temperature ninety-five degrees in the shade. Jane's sunsuit strap would usually be down over one shoulder, her blonde curls falling dankly over a damp forehead. Neither the temperature nor the season of the year had the slightest effect on Jane's ardor for this most favorite of all stories.

What she wanted was not some Yuletide fairy story but a detailed description of family Christmas activities, with the emphasis always on the four members of her family *doing something* together. She wanted a re-creation of the sights and colors, the sounds and, strangely, most of all the *smells* of Christmas: pine and balsam, open fires and candle wax, the fragrance of cookies and fruitcake and roasting turkey wafting from the kitchen. Jane's mother spent hours spinning many versions of this story. One little girl never tired of it. Just imagining Christmas at any time of the year put a glow of anticipation on her small face, seemed to satisfy some deep need of her childish heart.

The need the story spoke to was that deep human need for fellowship. "Doing something together" gives the feeling of closeness to other people as nothing else will.

I know just how Jane felt. When I was seven I came down with German measles. During convalescence my mother read to me that old juvenile, *The Five Little Peppers and How They Grew*. One passage in the book entranced me especially—the part about the Pepper family's Christmas.

Many years later I happened across the old book. Very curious as to why this one passage had such a halo around it in my memory, I reread the Christmas chapter. To my astonishment I found there was nothing very special about it. The Pepper children were very poor; they had to make their own ornaments. Bits of tin foil and bright paper were pasted over hickory nuts to hang on the tree. Candle ends were collected to light it. Polly and Ben Pepper popped popcorn, strung it and wove it in and out among the branches. Paper dolls and windmills were other ornaments.

How well I remember being almost envious of the Pepper family's poverty. What fun it would be, I thought, for a family to spend a whole evening together stringing popcorn and making ornaments.

Who wanted to buy Christmas tree ornaments? Who, indeed? Certainly no child.

This is something that children have taught me. For the over-privileged this takes self-control. For the underprivileged, it takes faith and imagination.

All children have that imagination, along with an ability to live in the present moment and a sharp sensitivity to a freshly beautiful world. It's as if a child savors life—sights, sounds, colors—fairly rolls it under his tongue. I never knew how dull of perception I had become until I saw Christmas through children's eyes. An icicle, a child told me, "had a rainbow in it" . . . Each fireplug wore "a cap of snow" . . . The winter lightning "looked like string beans dancing." One child was sure he had seen Santa's foot with a boot on it, just as he disappeared up the chimney. The comment of one tiny niece about the real reindeer imported at great expense for the children of Washington last Christmas was, "My, they smell awful!" Conversely, it was tiny Jane who made me aware again of the delectable smells of Christmas.

This renewed awareness of the joy of being alive, children have taught me. But we never learn any of this until we spend extra time with our children. They, in turn, need that extra time, if we really want to give them happiness and lastingly joyous memories at Christmas. My son Peter could never have made the toy chest without some suggestions and help. As a little girl I could never have made the trays without the aid of my parents. My father made the net for me with which I caught the butterflies; Mother tramped the woods with me and showed me how to press the ferns and wild flowers we gathered. It is a fact that the speed and artificiality of the life most of us are living these days, especially in our great cities, almost stifles the imaginative creativity of our children.

A friend of mine in a Southern city helped to develop a much-needed youth center. During the Christmas school holidays, part of the center's program was that the older young people invite a group of underprivileged children to spend a few days at the center.

They came. The young people and their advisers had planned what they thought would be fascinating activities for the youngsters. But all they wanted to do was to sit and read comic books. The leaders couldn't seem to break through to the children. The children did not seem to have the capacity to enjoy the activities.

My friend, whom I shall call Marjorie, loves children, and she knew that God loves them more than she does. She also had learned that no situation is ever hopeless. God always has creative ideas to give us for the asking, so, very simply, she asked Him to tell her how to get through to those boys and girls from the slums.

That evening after the children were in bed, Marjorie and several of the teen-agers were sitting, talking. All at once the inspired idea came. Marjorie looked across at her friend Peg and smiled. Peg had long blonde hair, at that moment screwed up in a quite unbecoming knot on top of her head.

"Peg, will you promise to do something for me? Unless you promise ahead of time, you'll probably try to wiggle out of it."

Peg hesitated. "Sounds ominous, but I'll try. What is it you want me to do?"

"Comb out your hair, put on that old blue evening dress from our trunk of costumes downstairs and be Mary for a Nativity scene in the woods back of the house. It's mild out. You won't freeze."

Peg's mouth dropped open as Marjorie outlined the plan. It was then nine-thirty. From then until one o'clock in the morning the group worked feverishly.

Shortly after one, each child was gently wakened and told, "We have seen something very exciting in the woods. We don't want you to miss it. Hurry! Slip on your shoes and coat. Don't say a word and follow me."

The sleepy, wondering youngsters were led toward the woods behind the recreation center. In one spot was Peg, with a blue scarf over her head, cradling the Infant Jesus; Joseph, one of the tall, teen-age boys, was nearby, resplendent in a multicolored bathrobe. A spotlight in a tall tree lighted the scene and gave it beauty. Farther on was Santa's workshop, with toys lying around. A melody from a music box tinkled through the woods. The children were allowed to look at the scenes only from a distance. In one spot three Christmas elves were holding a huge wooden bowl filled with onions from the kitchen. Even the onions looked entrancing. The children, by this time wide-eyed and amazed, were led back to bed.

"Slip into bed quietly. Don't talk and you may hear Santa's fairy flute. The fairies play it just once a year, around Christmastime." They heard it, all right. Far away on a hillside, through the night air, floated the thin, sweet, tinkling notes of the pipes. Marjorie had seen to that too.

"What did that do for the children?" I asked Marjorie.

"It was rather like breaking the sound barrier," she said. "It opened up something inside them—there all the time, but buried, inarticulate. The very next week they put on a winter carnival, with Roman candles and colored lights and a Snow Queen, as beautiful a thing as I've ever seen."

Yet without help this imaginative quality which is the mainspring of creativity would have stayed buried, and the children would have been content with reading comic books.

That is why the most cherished gift that we parents can give our children during the Yuletide season is our time—ourselves. No gift, no matter how expensive, can take the place of this.

What are some of the gifts time can bestow on our children? The chance to help them make the gifts they give away; a Christmas greens-cutting party, with the fun of cutting one's own tree; a Christmas bulletin board, on which are placed newspaper clippings of community Christmas events in which the family might be interested; a Christmas tree for the birds in the back yard; a cookie-making evening; a family evening of touring the outdoor Christmas trees and feasting on their beauty; much decorating of the house; evenings spent in wrapping especially imaginative packages; an evening at church listening to the beautiful music; the planning of a little family service to be held in the living room on Christmas morning. Time, much time—but our children will never forget a bit of it. Out of it will come deep and lasting satisfactions—the discovery of the joy of giving, a feeling of closeness to family and community.

And you too will reap untold dividends. In giving yourself completely to your children for this brief season, you too will find once again the happiness that comes only out of giving. For love springs from giving, even as giving grows out of love. Wherever love is, the Christ child eternally abides. May you find Him anew, for yourself and for your children, in your home and in your heart this Christmas.

Catherine Marshall

Vailima, June 19, 1891

I, Robert Louis Stevenson, Advocate of the Scots Bar, author of *The Master of Ballantrae* and *Moral Emblems,* stuck civil engineer, sole owner and patentee of the Palace and Plantation known as Vailima in the island of Upolu, Samoa, a British subject, being in sound mind, and pretty well, I thank you, in body:

In consideration that Miss Annie H. Ide, daughter of H. C. Ide, the town of Saint Johnsbury, in the county of Caledonia, in the state of Vermont, United States of America, was born, out of all reason, upon Christmas Day, and is therefore out of all justice denied the consolation and profit of a proper birthday;

And considering that I, the said Robert Louis Stevenson, have attained an age when O, we never mention it, and that I have now no further use for a birthday of any description;

And in consideration that I have met H. C. Ide, the father of the said Annie H. Ide, and found him about as white a land commissioner as I require:

Have transferred, and *do hereby transfer,* to the said Annie H. Ide, *all and whole* my rights and privileges in the thirteenth day of November, formerly my birthday, now, hereby, and henceforth, the birthday of the said Annie H. Ide, to have, hold, exercise, and enjoy the same in the customary manner, by the sporting of fine raiment, eating of rich meats, and receipt of gifts, compliments, and copies of verse, according to the manner of our ancestors;

And I direct the said Annie H. Ide to add to the said name of Annie H. Ide the name Louisa—at least in private; and I charge her to use my said birthday with moderation and humanity, *et tamquam bona filia familiae,* the said birthday not being so young as it once was, and having carried me in a very satisfactory manner since I can remember;

And in case the said Annie H. Ide shall neglect or contravene either of the above conditions, I hereby revoke the donation and transfer my rights in the said birthday to the President of the United States of America for the time being;

In witness whereof I have hereto set my hand and seal this nineteenth day of June in the year of grace eighteen hundred and ninety-one.

SEAL

Robert Louis Stevenson

Witness, *Lloyd Osbourne*
Witness, *Harold Watts*

YE GREAT ASTONISHMENT

Whosoever on ye nighte of ye nativity of ye young Lord Jesus, in ye great snows, shall fare forth bearing a succulent bone for ye loste and lamenting hounde, a whisp of hay for ye shivering horse, a cloak of warm raiment for ye stranded wayfarer, a bundle of fagots for ye twittering crone, a flagon of red wine for him whose marrow withers, a garland of bright berries for one who has worn chains, gay arias of lute and harp for all huddled birds who thought that song was dead, and divers lush sweetmeats for such babes' faces as peer from lonely windows—

To him shall be proffered and returned gifts of such an astonishment as will rival the hues of the peacock and the harmonies of heavens so that though he live to ye greate age when man goes stooping and querulous because of the nothing that is left in him, yet shall he walk upright and remembering, as one whose heart shines like a great star in his breasts.

Author Unknown

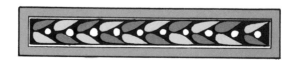

THE TWELVE DAYS OF CHRISTMAS

On the first day of Christmas
My true love sent to me
A partridge in a pear tree.

On the second day of Christmas
My true love sent to me
Two turtle doves, and
A partridge in a pear tree.

On the third day of Christmas
My true love sent to me
Three French hens,
Two turtle doves, and
A partridge in a pear tree.

On the fourth day of Christmas
My true love sent to me
Four colly birds,
Three French hens,
Two turtle doves, and
A partridge in a pear tree.

On the fifth day of Christmas
My true love sent to me
Five gold rings,
Four colly birds,
Three French hens,
Two turtle doves, and
A partridge in a pear tree.

On the sixth day of Christmas
My true love sent to me
Six geese a-laying,
Five gold rings,
Four colly birds,
Three French hens,
Two turtle doves, and
A partridge in a pear tree.

On the seventh day of Christmas
My true love sent to me
Seven swans a-swimming,
Six geese a-laying,
Five gold rings,
Four colly birds,
Three French hens,
Two turtle doves, and
A partridge in a pear tree.

On the eighth day of Christmas
My true love sent to me
Eight maids a-milking,
Seven swans a-swimming,
Six geese a-laying,
Five gold rings,
Four colly birds,
Three French hens,
Two turtle doves, and
A partridge in a pear tree.

On the ninth day of Christmas
My true love sent to me
Nine ladies dancing,
Eight maids a-milking,
Seven swans a-swimming,
Six geese a-laying,
Five gold rings,
Four colly birds,
Three French hens,
Two turtle doves, and
A partridge in a pear tree.

On the tenth day of Christmas
My true love sent to me
Ten lords a-leaping,
Nine ladies dancing,
Eight maids a-milking,
Seven swans a-swimming,
Six geese a-laying,
Five gold rings,
Four colly birds,
Three French hens,
Two turtle doves, and
A partridge in a pear tree.

On the eleventh day of Christmas
My true love sent to me
Eleven drummers drumming,
Ten lords a-leaping,
Nine ladies dancing,
Eight maids a-milking,
Seven swans a-swimming,
Six geese a-laying,
Five gold rings,
Four colly birds,
Three French hens,
Two turtle doves, and
A partridge in a pear tree.

On the twelfth day of Christmas
My true love sent to me
Twelve pipers piping,
Eleven drummers drumming,
Ten lords a-leaping,
Nine ladies dancing,
Eight maids a-milking,
Seven swans a-swimming,
Six geese a-laying,
Five gold rings,
Four colly birds,
Three French hens,
Two turtle doves, and
A partridge in a pear tree.

Traditional

CHANGE OF HEART

As the Advent season approaches and we celebrate again the coming of our Lord, I think it is time for us to prepare, as in the initial instance of His coming, for His appearance amongst us today. We are to be the herald or the evangel of the Good News, which begins with the announcement of Christ's coming. However, the message of Christ's arrival is always accompanied by a call to repentance. When we go back and study the Scriptures of the announcement that was made to Mary, when Mary received the word that she was to bear the Son of God, she proclaimed the Hymn of praise—the Magnificat—which reads in part:

"He has shown strength with His arm, He has scattered the proud in the imagination of their hearts, He has put down the mighty from their thrones, and exalted those of low degree; He has filled the hungry with good things, and the rich He has sent away empty" (Luke 1:51–53).

We see that the call for repentance and for radical change within society is interwoven with the proclamation of the coming of the Lord. The political and social implications of the incarnation are present from the very moment of Christ's conception within Mary.

We see this same truth at the birth of Christ. Matthew tells us that when Christ was just an infant, He was already viewed as a threat by the political and religious establishment. King Herod took the word of foreign astrologers so seriously, and was so fearful of one who would call into question his power and his authority, that he ordered a massacre of infants. As a baby, Jesus and His parents fled from their land because of political persecution.

If we study the Gospels carefully, we see that there is no foundation for assuming that the true spiritual significance of Christ as Messiah and as our Savior in any way negates the radical, political and social consequences of His incarnation, His life, His death and His resurrection. We see that in the words of John the Baptist, who as the preparer of the way of the Lord called for social repentance, individual and corporate:

"A voice crying aloud in the wilderness, 'Prepare a way for the Lord; clear a straight path for Him. Every ravine shall be filled in, and every mountain and hill leveled; the corners shall be straightened, and the rough ways made smooth; and all mankind shall see God's deliverance' " (Luke 3:4–6).

In this beautiful melding of the Old Testament scriptures with the New, John the Baptist warned of God's judgment of the injustice of society. He also condemned the "establishment"; when he saw many of the Pharisees and Sadducees coming for baptism, he said to them:

116

" 'You vipers' brood! Who warned you to escape from the coming retribution? Then prove your repentance by the fruit it bears' " (Matt. 3:7–8). His message also continued: "Already the axe is laid to the roots of the trees; and every tree that fails to produce good fruit is cut down and thrown on the fire' " (v. 10).

So the awareness of Christ's appearance—the Word made flesh—results in proclaiming a call to individual repentance and to social repentance. Therefore, I believe that . . . a part of being an evangelist and proclaiming the good news of Christ's life is issuing this call for repentance.

Now modern calls to repentance sound a bit foreign, even in some theological circles, because as a people we have nearly lost the social and individual awareness of sin. The prophets who called for repentance and warned of God's judgment within previous citadels of corruption spent most of their time trying to get a society to recognize its own sin. In Egypt, in Nineveh, in Sodom and Gomorrah, in the forty years in the wilderness, in Jerusalem, in pagan Rome, in the Holy Roman Empire and in modern nations prophets have tried to make people aware of their sins. They have called upon people to turn from their wicked ways; but the problem is that people living in the midst of sin usually fail to recognize their own true condition.

Modern America has nearly lost any capacity for corporate repentance, because it has so thoroughly evaded any awareness of corporate sin.

Likewise, the modern American finds any call to individual repentance strange and out of date for he has generally discarded any relevant understanding of individual sin. This is also reflected in the erosion of personal accountability. We have gained in our modern day much valuable insight from the social sciences about what influences human behavior. Sociology, psychology, psychiatry, human genetics, and other academic disciplines have all enabled us to discover much about the human personality. But there is a tendency for social science to attempt a comprehensive explanation of every human action. The result can be the diminishing and the loss of personal accountability. Generally, we try to avoid becoming individually answerable for wrongdoings on our part. We explain it away on the system, or on circumstances we couldn't control, or that we were just following orders, or that the guilt of others has wrongly tinged ourselves. [However,] Dr. Karl Menninger, . . . a psychiatrist, [has written]: "There is immorality. There is unethical behavior. There is wrongdoing. And I hope to show that there is usefulness in retaining the concept and indeed the word, sin."

Menninger claims that recovering the proper, healthy recognition of personal accountability and of sin is essential for bringing people and society to a state of health. This does not mean the legalistic, self-righteous moralizing that only builds up false guilt in people. Rather it means the compassionate understanding that there is always the element of human freedom, and the ability to transcend one's own personal ego and do what is right, and what is loving, as opposed to what is wrong, unloving and sinful.

Social conformity can become another means of escaping the awareness of individual sin. We believe that society is the best dictate of morality, and we are doing nothing wrong if we are acting like everyone else. And many times we can say with accuracy the church has become inculturated where it reflects the values of society rather than influencing those values. The Christian call to repentance questions and rejects the values and standards of existing society. It sets forth, as the Christian call, a Person as the standard for our radical

allegiance. In judging society, He calls us to live according to a new order, to turn away from sin and have our lives redirected and remade. So our message must recover the modern relevance of individual personal sin and personal accountability. . . .

In my opinion, American civil religion has blinded us to our national sin. It has dulled our sensitivity to the need for corporate repentance, because a characteristic of our civil religion is that it has created myths about America as sort of a modern chosen people of God; that Washington like Moses was leading the people out of bondage to a promised land; and that the Constitution and the Declaration of Independence were written after inspired prayer meetings. "In God We Trust" is on money, of all things. God is invoked to bless us, to lead us, to bring us to victory. The relationship between the state and faith is totally destroyed in this kind of religion. because in this instance, religion is used to justify and to sanctify the status quo. The state and its rulers invoke a divine mandate.

I think the problem began with Constantine. He co-opted the church. My belief is that he used the trappings of Christianity and Christendom to support his own political ends and to advance the Empire. But interestingly, that pattern has been repeated many times in history. And perhaps it is what we face today. If we believe in the God of an American civil religion, our faith is in a small and a very exclusive deity, a loyal spiritual advisor to American power and prestige, an exclusive defender of the American nation, and the object of a national folk religion that is devoid of moral content. Our civil religion places our nation beyond sin and above judgment. It baptizes nationalistic vainglory. We abdicate our individual responsibility and the dictates of our personal faith to corporate idolatry. We can see this both in the religious realm where the integrity of our faith is compromised by civil religion and politically when idolatry of power overcomes individual convictions.

We must recover a vivid awareness of our corporate sin as a nation and as a people. I believe that our nation will never recover its health or hold out any promise for renewal, unless we can face our darkness, our corruption, our sin. It is a dangerous pathological sickness for an individual or a nation to be utterly blind to inner failings and wrong and to believe that all of one's actions can be vindicated and are utterly righteous. "If we refuse to admit that we are sinners, we live in a world of illusion, and truth becomes a stranger to us," as St. John records.

Our evangelism today must provide a meaningful sense of repentance, individual and corporate. We must build an evangelical thrust that fully relates to our modern sins of both omission and commission. We must not think that our evangelical task can be carried out in some kind of social or political vacuum. The word was made flesh. Christ came to a real world of political upheaval, social turmoil, human suffering and spiritual blindness. His life and His ministry were relevant to all those situations. And therefore, the sharing of His life must be related to all these conditions as they are in our society today. We must see what we are to be saved *from* and what we are redeemed and liberated by Christ *for*. The false dichotomy between the personal and the social must be destroyed. The notion that being evangelical means that one does not have to concern himself with social problems, or that ministering to social ills is different from an evangelical concern is simply heretical, whichever way you look at it. I believe our task is to restore the whole Gospel. Sin is both corporate and personal, and usually both at the same time. The coming of Christ speaks both to our personal lives and to our corporate structures, just as it did in Palestine 2,000 years ago.

Let us examine our contemporary sins and the requirements for repentance today. There are many ways you can list them. This is not an exclusive list, but let me begin with war, violence, nationalism, and militarism. Christ came as the Prince of Peace. And in the words of the prophet quoted by Zechariah, father of John the Baptist, He came "to guide our feet into the way of peace" (Luke 1:79).

Yet today we are beset with the psychology of war. We are overladen with the means of war. We are addicted to the ways of war. We are enslaved to a belief in war. All of this arises out of our own attitudes. It is nourished by our individual hatreds, our individual violence. Alexander Solzhenitsyn said, "Violence is brazenly and victoriously striding across the whole world. There was a time when violence was a means of last resort. Now it is a method of communication."

. . . Whenever we hear and accept the admonitions about being the most powerful nation on earth, being number one in all we do, and achieving a "peace with honor," then the attitudes of national exaltation and righteousness becomes further ingrained as the justification for our power and violence. Arnold Toynbee has written: "Nationalism is the real religion today of a majority of people. . . . How can we arrive at a lasting peace? . . . For a true and lasting peace, religious revolution is a 'sine qua non.' By religion, I mean the overcoming of self-centeredness in both individuals and communities, by getting into communion with the spiritual presence behind the universe. . . . Until we do, the survival of the human race will continue to be in doubt."

Faith in Christ imparts to all of us this vision of our humanity. Paul writes in Colossians that Christ by His death on the cross has created a new humanity, has reconciled all men as one. There is no distinction, no difference, no division between Jew and Gentile, Greek and slave, free and foreigner and all—no distinction because Christ lives in them all. Without elaborate exegesis it is plain that Paul does not just mean that all acknowledged believers are one, but that all men are one. Christ brought about the unity of mankind. "If any one is in Christ, he is a new creation" (II Cor. 5:17). So repentance today must include a call to turn from hatreds, personal and corporate, which have divided us from others so we can be remade by Christ's love for us and for all mankind.

In our nation we also have the sin of poverty. The poorest one-fifth of families in America receive only five percent of our nation's total family income. The wealthiest one-fifth of our society in America receive forty-two percent of the total family income. This fact, my friends, has not changed in twenty-five years. Economists will have a lot of names and explanations for the existence of poverty in an affluent society, but biblically, there is one simple term to describe this reality and that is sin. Continuously, the Bible regards poverty in the midst of plenty as sin. That is the case for our own day in our own society. We are now approaching a one-trillion-dollar gross national product and yet there are still hundreds of thousands, even millions in our land who are hungry, who are improperly nourished, who live with rats in shacks, who cannot afford medical care, and who are afflicted with all the disabilities of opportunity and knowledge that poverty brings in this society.

What was the greatest sin of Sodom? What was it that caused its destruction by God? Sexual immorality? Read the words of Ezekiel: "This was the iniquity of your sister Sodom. She and her daughters had pride of wealth and food in plenty, comfort and ease and yet she never helped the poor and the wretched."

Our modern call to repentance must cause us to repent from the sin of neglecting the poor, both as a nation and as individuals.

Another related sin is our materialism, our economic idols. Our

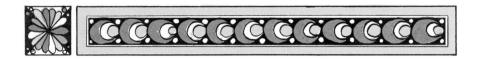

wealth and our ever-increasing affluence constitute a sin involving each of our lives, and sin that is compounding the crisis in our society. Christ warns us again and again about the dangers of wealth. He says that we cannot serve God and the power of money. He speaks about the difficulty of the rich man ever entering the Kingdom of God. He tells us not to worry about what we are to eat, drink and wear. As one example in Luke, Christ says, " 'Beware of the lawyers who love to walk up and down in long robes, and have a great liking for respectful greetings in the street, the chief seats in our synagogues, and places of honor at feasts. These are the men who eat up the property of widows, while they say long prayers for appearance' sake; and they will receive the severest sentence' " (Luke 20:45–47). We live in a society that totally serves mammon, the power of money, the "almighty dollar." Thoughtlessly we can be carried along by those values, those commitments and those priorities that serve the world, rather than our Lord. . . .

We need in our society, and in the light of the Gospel, that kind of perspective as a part of our call to repentance. Our wealth and our standard of living are causes of endless other problems such as our energy crisis, the ruining of our physical environment, and our outright monopoly on the world's basic resources, but at its heart, such wealth simply manifests corporate selfishness, and individual self-centeredness. As such, it is another example of sin.

There are other sins that abound in our modern society which we could examine—lying, stealing, cheating, taking what is not one's own, and all the contemporary forms of narcotic self-indulgence. These are sins that go on at all levels of society, in our corporations, in our finest schools, in our churches and everywhere else. Included are all of the compromises with integrity which are so easily rationalized in our contemporary life in the name of getting ahead or building a reputation or not rocking the boat or just doing one's job, or "to get along, you go along." In all of these matters we have discussed we must confront anew the reality of sin—social sin and personal sin interwoven together.

In every case, what is called for is a change of heart—for people to turn around, to be converted, to receive the Good News, to be forgiven, to be accepted, to encounter Christ. And in each case we are called to a renewal of society, to corporate repentance, to justice, to

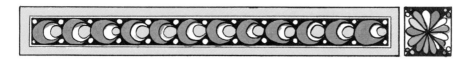

relief of the suffering, "to proclaim the release of the captives, to set at liberty those who are oppressed," as the Scripture states. That must be the shape of the evangelistic mission in our time and our land.

. . . The one last area where our message must be applied is in the way our society and we as individuals worship power. This is particularly true in the political realm. But it holds true for power in the university or in the church or in any other institution. We tend to idolize power. When people gain great power, they then frequently think of themselves as idols. Power can make one totally self-centered.

. . . It massages the prima-donna complex in a person. To keep our power, we are taught by political wisdom to believe that we must always justify ourselves to others and that we can never admit an error or never admit wrong. Confession becomes equated with weakness, so one comes to believe that he is immune from normal human fallibilities. He places himself even above the law in this self-exultation. So power is held and clung to by any means, defended at any cost, in order to maintain one's very identity. And once again we must see that sin is in this kind of psychology and this kind of action. There must be reestablished in the areas of political leadership the element of personal accountabilities. Without the ability to admit error and wrongdoing, power becomes tyrannical.

The style of leadership that we can emulate is again seen in the person of the Lord. Our society must come to see the whole new vision of leadership. We must understand that leadership is not the protection of power, but rather the commitment to service. There must be an ultimate commitment to the truth, whether in Christian fellowship or the political realm. When the truth or the word of God is shared as a common possession, then there is unity. But when truth is withheld, and defined only by one claiming a higher prerogative, then there are division, suspicion and mistrust. The commitment of leadership as seen in the life of Christ is to service, rather than to self-maintenance. It is an openness, a candor, a humility, a sacrifice. It places the well-being of the other ahead of his own. Christ tells us if we are to save our lives, we must give our lives away.

Political wisdom of the day teaches precisely the opposite—to save one's life, he takes, he squeezes, he grabs, he accumulates, he surrounds himself with protection.

What is required in this aspect of repentance is a whole new understanding of leadership and power, one which is just the opposite of what our society would have us believe.

Again, in Luke we hear Christ say: "'In the world, kings lord it over their subjects; . . . Not so with you . . . I am among you like a servant'" (Luke 22:25–27). We must turn from this idolatry of power to the vision of one who is a servant leader. Then we can see a new leadership that is defined and exemplified by sacrificial service rather than the maintenance of power, marked by humility, openness and compassion. And the prophetic vision of Christ's first coming proclaimed by Mary can be realized anew in our time. "He has scattered the proud in the imagination of their hearts, He has put down the mighty from their thrones, and exalted those of low degree" (Luke 1:51–52).

Mark O. Hatfield, United States Senator from Oregon

MY GIFT

What can I give Him
Poor as I am;
If I were a shepherd,
I would give Him a lamb.
If I were a wise man,
I would do my part.
But what can I give Him?
I will give Him my heart.
Christina G. Rossetti

THE JOY OF GIVING

Somehow not only for Christmas
But all the long year through,
The joy that you give to others
Is the joy that comes back to you.

And the more you spend in blessing
The poor and lonely and sad,
The more of your heart's possessing
Returns to make you glad.
John Greenleaf Whittier

Christmas is coming, the geese are getting
  fat,
Please to put a penny in the old man's hat;
If you haven't got a penny, a ha'penny will do,
If you haven't got a ha'penny, God bless you!
Beggar's Rhyme

Christmas is a time for "giving up" sin, bad habits, and selfish pleasures. Christmas is a time for "giving in" surrender to Christ, ac-
ceptance of Him as King. Christmas is a time for "giving out" real
giving, not swapping.

Anonymous

From A CHRISTMAS CAROL

Stave Four The Last of the Spirits

The Phantom slowly, gravely, silently, approached. When it came near him, Scrooge bent down upon his knee, for in the very air through which this spirit moved it seemed to scatter gloom and mystery.

It was shrouded in a deep black garment, which concealed its head, its face, its form, and left nothing of it visible save one out-stretched hand. But for this it would have been difficult to detach its figure from the night, and separate it from the darkness by which it was surrounded.

He felt that it was tall and stately when it came beside him, and that its mysterious presence filled him with a solemn dread. He knew no more, for the Spirit neither spoke nor moved.

"I am in the presence of the Ghost of Christmas Yet to Come?" said Scrooge.

The Spirit answered not, but pointed onward with its hand.

"You are about to show me shadows of the things that have not happened, but will happen in the time before us," Scrooge pursued. "Is that so, Spirit?"

The upper portion of the garment was contracted for an instant in its folds, as if the Spirit had inclined its head. That was the only answer he received.

Although well used to ghostly company by this time, Scrooge feared the silent shape so much that his legs trembled beneath him, and he found that he could hardly stand when he prepared to follow it. The Spirit paused a moment, as if observing his condition, and giving him time to recover.

But Scrooge was all the worse for this. It thrilled him with a vague uncertain horror, to know that, behind the dusky shroud, there were ghostly eyes intently fixed upon him, while he, though he stretched his own to the utmost, could see nothing but a spectral hand and one great heap of black.

"Ghost of the Future!" he exclaimed, "I fear you more than any specter I have seen. But as I know your purpose is to do me good, and as I hope to live to be another man from what I was, I am prepared to bear you company, and do it with a thankful heart. Will you not speak to me?"

It gave him no reply. The hand was pointed straight before them.

"Lead on!" said Scrooge—"lead on! The night is waning fast, and it is precious time to me, I know. Lead on, Spirit!"

The Phantom moved away as it had come toward him. Scrooge followed in the shadow of its dress, which bore him up, he thought, and carried him along.

They scarcely seemed to enter the City, for the City rather seemed to spring up about them, and encompass them of its own act. But there they were, in the heart of it, on 'Change, among the merchants, who hurried up and down, and chinked the money in their pockets, and conversed in groups, and looked at their watches, and trifled thoughtfully with their great gold seals, and so forth, as Scrooge had seen them often.

The Spirit stopped beside one little knot of business men. Observing that the hand was pointed to them, Scrooge advanced to listen to their talk.

"No," said a great fat man with a monstrous chin, "I don't know much about it either way. I only know he's dead."

"When did he die?" inquired another.

"Last night, I believe."

"Why, what was the matter with him?" asked a third, taking a vast quantity of snuff out of a very large snuff-box. "I thought he'd never die."

"God knows," said the first, with a yawn.

"What has he done with his money?" asked a red-faced gentleman with a pendulous excrescence on the end of his nose, that shook like the gills of a turkey-cock.

"I haven't heard," said the man with the large chin, yawning again. "Left it to his company, perhaps. He hasn't left it to *me*. That's all I know."

This pleasantry was received with a general laugh.

"It's likely to be a very cheap funeral," said the same speaker, "for, upon my life, I don't know of anybody to go to it. Suppose we make up a party, and volunteer?"

"I don't mind going if a lunch is provided," observed the gentleman with the excrescence on his nose. "But I must be fed, if I make one."

Another laugh.

"Well, I am the most disinterested among you, after all," said the first speaker, "for I never wear black gloves, and I never eat lunch. But I'll offer to go, if anybody else will. When I come to think of it, I'm not at all sure that I wasn't his most particular friend, for we used to stop and speak whenever we met. By-by!"

Speakers and listeners strolled away, and mixed with other groups. Scrooge knew the men, and looked toward the Spirit for an explanation.

The Phantom glided on into a street. Its finger pointed to two persons meeting. Scrooge listened again, thinking that the explanation might lie here.

He knew these men, also, perfectly. They were men of business, very wealthy, and of great importance. He had made a point always of standing well in their esteem—in a business point of view, that is, strictly in a business point of view.

"How are you?" said one.

"How are you?" returned the other.

"Well!" said the first. "Old Scratch has got his own at last, hey?"

"So I am told," returned the second. "Cold, isn't it?"

"Seasonable for Christmas-time. You are not a skater, I suppose?"

"No. No. Something else to think of. Good morning!"

Not another word. That was their meeting, their conversation, and their parting.

Scrooge was at first inclined to be surprised that the Spirit should attach importance to conversations apparently so trivial, but feeling assured that they must have some hidden purpose, he set himself to consider what it was likely to be. They could scarcely be supposed to have any bearing on the death of Jacob, his old partner, for that was Past, and this Ghost's province was the Future. Nor could he think of any one immediately connected with himself, to whom he could apply them. But nothing doubting that, to whomsoever they applied, they had some latent moral for his own improvement, he resolved to treasure up every word he heard, and everything he saw, and especially to observe the shadow of himself when it appeared. For he had an expectation that the conduct of his future self would give him the clue he missed, and would render the solution of these riddles easy.

He looked about in that very place for his own image, but another man stood in his accustomed corner, and though the clock pointed to his usual time of day for being there, he saw no likeness of himself among the multitudes that poured in through the Porch. It gave him little surprise, however, for he had been revolving in his mind a change of life, and thought and hoped he saw his newborn resolutions carried out in this.

Quiet and dark, beside him stood the Phantom, with its outstretched hand. When he roused himself from his thoughtful quest, he fancied, from the turn of the hand and its situation in reference to himself, that the Unseen Eyes were looking at him keenly. It made him shudder, and feel very cold.

They left the busy scene, and went into an obscure part of the town, where Scrooge had never penetrated before, although he recognized its situation, and its bad repute. The ways were foul and narrow, the shops and houses wretched, the people half naked, drunken, slipshod, ugly. Alleys and archways, like so many cesspools, disgorged their offenses of smell, and dirt, and life, upon the straggling streets; and the whole quarter reeked with crime, with filth and misery.

Far in this den of infamous resort, there was a low-browed, beetling shop, below a pent-house roof, where iron, old rags, bottles, bones, and greasy offal were bought. Upon the floor within were piled up heaps of rusty keys, nails, chains, hinges, files, scales, weights, and refuse iron of all kinds. Secrets that few would like to scrutinize were bred and hidden in mountains of unseemly rags, masses of corrupted fat, and sepulchers of bones. Sitting in among the wares he dealt in, by a charcoal stove, made of old bricks, was a gray-haired rascal, nearly seventy years of age, who had screened himself from the cold air without by a frowzy curtaining of miscellaneous tatters, hung upon a line, and smoked his pipe in all the luxury of calm retirement.

Scrooge and the Phantom came into the presence of this man, just as a woman with a heavy bundle slunk into the shop. But she had scarcely entered, when another woman, similarly laden, came in too, and she was closely followed by a man in faded black, who was no less startled by the sight of them than they had been upon the recognition of each other. After a short period of blank astonishment, in which the old man with the pipe had joined them, they all three burst into a laugh.

"Let the charwoman alone to be the first!" cried she who had entered first. "Let the laundress alone to be the second, and let the undertaker's man alone to be the third. Look here, old Joe, here's a chance! If we haven't all three met here without meaning it!"

"You couldn't have met in a better place," said old Joe, removing his pipe from his mouth. "Come into the parlor. You were made free of it long ago, you know, and the other two ain't strangers. Stop till I shut the door of the shop. Ah! How it shreeks! There ain't such a rusty bit of metal in the place as its own hinges, I believe, and I'm sure there's no such old bones here as mine. Ha, ha! We're all suitable to our calling, we're well matched. Come into the parlor. Come into the parlor."

The parlor was the space behind the screen of rags. The old man raked the fire together with an old stair-rod, and having trimmed his smoky lamp (for it was night) with the stem of his pipe, put it in his mouth again.

While he did this, the woman who had already spoken threw her bundle on the floor, and sat down in a flaunting manner on a stool, crossing her elbows on her knees, and looking with a bold defiance at the other two.

"What odds, then? What odds, Mrs. Dilber?" said the woman. "Every person has a right to take care of themselves. *He* always did!"

"That's true, indeed!" said the laundress. "No man more so."

"Why, then, don't stand staring as if you was afraid, woman! Who's the wiser? We're not going to pick holes in each other's coats, I suppose?"

"No, indeed!" said Mrs. Dilber and the man together. "We should hope not."

"Very well, then!" cried the woman. "That's enough. Who's the worse for the loss of a few things like these? Not a dead man, I suppose?"

"No, indeed," said Mrs. Dilber, laughing.

"If he wanted to keep 'em after he was dead, a wicked old screw," pursued the woman, "why wasn't he natural in his lifetime? If he had been, he'd have had somebody to look after him when he was struck with Death, instead of lying gasping out his last there, alone by himself."

"It's the truest word that ever was spoke," said Mrs. Dilber. "It's a judgment on him."

"I wish it was a little heavier judgment," replied the woman, "and it should have been, you may depend upon it, if I could have laid my hands on anything else. Open that bundle, old Joe, and let me know the value of it. Speak out plain. I'm not afraid to be the first, nor afraid for them to see it. We knew pretty well that we were helping ourselves, before we met here, I believe. It's no sin. Open the bundle, Joe."

But the gallantry of her friends would not allow of this, and the man in faded black, mounting the breach first, produced *his* plunder. It was not extensive. A seal or two, a pencil-case, a pair of sleeve-buttons, and a brooch of no great value, were all. They were severally examined and appraised by old Joe, who chalked the sums he was disposed to give for each upon the wall, and added them up into a total when he found that there was nothing more to come.

"That's your account," said Joe, "and I wouldn't give another sixpence, if I was to be boiled for not doing it. Who's next?"

Mrs. Dilber was next. Sheets and towels, a little wearing-apparel, two old-fashioned silver teaspoons, a pair of sugar-tongs, and a few boots. Her account was stated on the wall in the same manner.

"I always give too much to ladies. Its a weakness of mine, and that's the way I ruin myself," said old Joe. "That's your account. If you asked me for another penny, and made it an open question, I'd repent of being so liberal, and knock off half a crown."

"And now undo *my* bundle, Joe," said the first woman.

Joe went down on his knees for the greater convenience of opening it, and, having unfastened a great many knots, dragged out a large, heavy roll of some dark stuff.

"What do you call this?" said Joe. "Bed-curtains?"

"Ah!" returned the woman, laughing and leaning forward on her crossed arms. "Bed-curtains!"

"You don't mean to say you took 'em down, rings and all, with him lying there?" said Joe.

"Yes, I do," replied the woman. "Why not?"

"You were born to make your fortune," said Joe, "and you'll certainly do it."

"I certainly sha'n't hold my hand, when I can get anything in it by reaching it out, for the sake of such a man as He was, I promise you, Joe," returned the woman coolly. "Don't drop that oil upon the blankets now."

"His blankets?" asked Joe.

"Whose else's do you think?" replied the woman. "He isn't likely to take cold without 'em, I dare say."

"I hope he didn't die of anything catching? Eh?" said old Joe, stopping in his work, and looking up.

"Don't be afraid of that," returned the woman. "I ain't so fond of his company that I'd loiter about him for such things, if he did. Ah!

You may look through that shirt till your eyes ache; but you won't find a hole in it, nor a threadbare place. It's the best he had, and a fine one too. They'd have wasted it, if it hadn't been for me."

"What do you call wasting of it?" asked old Joe.

"Putting it on him to be buried in, to be sure," replied the woman, with a laugh. "Somebody was fool enough to do it, but I took it off again. If calico ain't good enough for such a purpose, it isn't good enough for anything. It's quite as becoming to the body. He can't look uglier than he did in that one."

Scrooge listened to this dialogue in horror. As they sat grouped about their spoil, in the scanty light afforded by the old man's lamp, he viewed them with a detestation and disgust which could hardly have been greater though they had been obscene demons, marketing the corpse itself.

"Ha, ha!" laughed the same woman, when old Joe, producing a flannel bag with money in it, told out their several gains upon the ground. "This is the end of it, you see! He frightened every one away from him when he was alive, to profit us when he was dead! Ha, ha, ha!"

"Spirit!" said Scrooge, shuddering from head to foot. "I see, I see. The case of this unhappy man might be my own. My life tends that way now. Merciful Heaven, what is this?"

He recoiled in terror, for the scene had changed, and now he almost touched a bed—a bare, uncurtained bed, on which, beneath a ragged sheet, there lay a something covered up, which, though it was dumb, announced itself in awful language.

The room was very dark, too dark to be observed with any accuracy, though Scrooge glanced round it in obedience to a secret impulse, anxious to know what kind of room it was. A pale light, rising in the outer air, fell straight upon the bed, and on it, plundered and bereft, unwatched, unwept, uncared for, was the body of this man.

Scrooge glanced toward the Phantom. Its steady hand was pointed to the head. The cover was so carelessly adjusted that the slightest raising of it, the motion of a finger upon Scrooge's part, would have disclosed the face. He thought of it, felt how easy it would be to do, and longed to do it, but had no more power to withdraw the veil than to dismiss the specter at his side.

Oh cold, cold, rigid, dreadful Death, set up thine altar here, and dress it with such terrors as thou hast at thy command, for this is thy dominion! But of the loved, revered, and honored head, thou canst not turn one hair to thy dread purposes, or make one feature odious. It is not that the hand is heavy, and will fall down when released; it is not that the heart and pulse are still: but that the hand was open, generous, and true, the heart brave, warm, and tender, and the pulse

a man's. Strike, Shadow, strike! And see his good deeds springing from the wound, to sow the world with life immortal!

No voice pronounced these words in Scrooge's ears, and yet he heard them when he looked upon the bed. He thought, if this man could be raised up now, what would be his foremost thoughts? Avarice, hard dealing, griping cares? They have brought him to a rich end, truly!

He lay, in the dark, empty house, with not a man, a woman, or a child to say he was kind to me in this or that, and for the memory of one kind word I will be kind to him. A cat was tearing at the door, and there was a sound of gnawing rats beneath the hearthstone. What *they* wanted in the room of death, and why they were so restless and disturbed, Scrooge did not dare to think.

"Spirit!" he said, "this is a fearful place. In leaving it, I shall not leave its lesson, trust me. Let us go!"

Still the Ghost pointed with an unmoved finger to the head.

"I understand you," Scrooge returned, "and I would do it, if I could. But I have not the power, Spirit. I have not the power."

Again it seemed to look upon him.

"If there is any person in the town who feels emotion caused by this man's death," said Scrooge, quite agonized, "show that person to me, Spirit. I beseech you!"

The Phantom spread its dark robe before him for a moment, like a wing and withdrawing it, revealed a room by daylight, where a mother and her children were.

She was expecting some one, and with anxious eagerness: for she walked up and down the room, started at every sound, looked out from the window, glanced at the clock, tried, but in vain, to work with her needle, and could hardly bear the voices of her children in their play.

At length the long-expected knock was heard. She hurried to the door, and met her husband, a man whose face was care-worn and depressed, though he was young. There was a remarkable expression in it now, a kind of serious delight of which he felt ashamed, and which he struggled to repress.

He sat down to the dinner that had been hoarding for him by the fire, and when she asked him faintly what news (which was not until after a long silence), he appeared embarrassed how to answer.

"Is it good," she said, "or bad?"—to help him.

"Bad," he answered.

"We are quite ruined?"

"No. There is hope yet, Caroline."

"If *he* relents," said she, amazed, "there is! Nothing is past hope, if such a miracle has happened."

"He is past relenting," said her husband. "He is dead."

She was a mild and patient creature, if her face spoke truth; but she was thankful in her soul to hear it, and she said so, with clasped hands. She prayed forgiveness the next moment, and was sorry, but the first was the emotion of her heart.

"What the half-drunken woman whom I told you of last night said to me, when I tried to see him and obtain a week's delay, and what I thought was a mere excuse to avoid me, turns out to have been quite true. He was not only very ill, but dying, then."

"To whom will our debt be transferred?"

"I don't know. But before that time we shall be ready with the money and even though we were not, it would be bad fortune indeed to find so merciless a creditor in his successor. We may sleep to-night with light hearts, Caroline!"

Yes. Soften it as they would, their hearts were lighter. The children's faces, hushed and clustered round to hear what they so little understood, were brighter, and it was a happier house for this man's death! The only emotion that the Ghost could show him, caused by the event, was one of pleasure.

"Let me see some tenderness connected with a death," said Scrooge, "or that dark chamber, Spirit, which we left just now will be forever present to me."

The Ghost conducted him through several streets familiar to his feet and, as they went along, Scrooge looked here and there to find himself, but nowhere was he to be seen. They entered poor Bob Cratchit's house—the dwelling he had visited before—and found the mother and the children seated round the fire.

Quiet. Very quiet. The noisy little Cratchits were as still as statues in one corner, and sat looking up at Peter, who had a book before him. The mother and her daughters were engaged in sewing. But surely they were very quiet!

"'And he took a child, and set him in the midst of them.'"

Where had Scrooge heard those words? He had not dreamed them. The boy must have read them out, as he and the Spirit crossed the threshold. Why did he not go on?

The mother laid her work upon the table, and put her hand up to her face.

"The color hurts my eyes," she said.

The color? Ah, poor Tiny Tim!

"They're better now again," said Cratchit's wife. "It makes them weak by candle-light; and I wouldn't show weak eyes to your father when he comes home, for the world. It must be near his time."

"Past it, rather," Peter answered, shutting up his book. "But I think he has walked a little slower than he used, these few last evenings, mother."

They were very quiet again. At last she said, and in a steady, cheerful voice, that only faltered once:

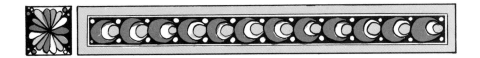

"I have known him walk with—I have known him walk with Tiny Tim upon his shoulder very fast indeed."

"And so have I," cried Peter. "Often."

"And so have I," exclaimed another. So had all.

"But he was very light to carry," she resumed, intent upon her work, "and his father loved him so, that it was no trouble—no trouble. And there is your father at the door!"

She hurried out to meet him, and little Bob in his comforter—he had need of it, poor fellow—came in. His tea was ready for him on the hob, and they all tried who should help him to it most. Then the two young Cratchits got upon his knees, and laid, each child, a little cheek against his face, as if they said, "Don't mind it, father. Don't be grieved!"

Bob was very cheerful with them, and spoke pleasantly to all the family. He looked at the work upon the table, and praised the industry and speed of Mrs. Cratchit and the girls. They would be done long before Sunday, he said.

"Sunday! You went to-day, then, Robert?" said his wife.

"Yes, my dear," returned Bob. "I wish you could have gone. It would have done you good to see how green a place it is. But you'll see it often. I promised him that I would walk there on a Sunday. My little, little child!" cried Bob. "My little child!"

He broke down all at once. He couldn't help it. If he could have helped it, he and his child would have been farther apart, perhaps, than they were.

He left the room, and went up-stairs into the room above, which was lighted cheerfully, and hung with Christmas. There was a chair set close beside the child, and there were signs of some one having been there lately. Poor Bob sat down in it, and when he had thought a little and composed himself, he kissed the little face. He was reconciled to what had happened, and went down again quite happy.

They drew about the fire and talked, the girls and mother working still. Bob told them of the extraordinary kindness of Mr. Scrooge's nephew, whom he had scarcely seen but once, and who, meeting him in the street that day, and seeing that he looked a little—"just a little down, you know," said Bob, inquired what had happened to distress him. "On which," said Bob, "for he is the pleasantest-spoken gentleman you ever heard, I told him. 'I am heartily sorry for it, Mr.

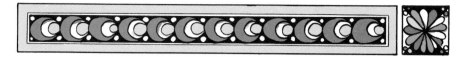

Cratchit,' he said, 'and heartily sorry for your good wife.' By the by, how he ever knew *that*, I don't know."

"Knew what, my dear?"

"Why, that you were a good wife," replied Bob.

"Everybody knows that," said Peter.

"Very well observed, my boy!" cried Bob. "I hope they do. 'Heartily sorry,' he said, 'for your good wife. If I can be of service to you in any way,' he said, giving me his card, 'that's where I live. Pray to come to me.' Now it wasn't," cried Bob, "for the sake of any-thing he might be able to do for us, so much as for his kind way, that this was quite delightful. It really seemed as if he had known our Tiny Tim, and felt with us."

"I'm sure he's a good soul!" said Mrs. Cratchit.

"You would be sure of it, my dear," returned Bob, "if you saw and spoke to him. I shouldn't be at all surprised—mark what I say!—if he got Peter a better situation."

"Only hear that, Peter," said Mrs. Cratchit.

"And then," cried one of the girls, "Peter will be keeping com-pany with some one, and setting up for himself."

"Get along with you!" retorted Peter, grinning.

"It's just as likely as not," said Bob, "one of these days, though there's plenty of time for that, my dear. But, however and whenever we part from one another, I am sure we shall none of us forget poor Tiny Tim—shall we?—or this first parting that there was among us?"

"Never, father!" cried they all.

"And I know," said Bob—"I know, my dears, that when we recol-lect how patient and how mild he was, although he was a little, little child, we shall not quarrel easily among ourselves, and forget poor Tiny Tim in doing it."

"No, never, father!" they all cried again.

"I am very happy," said little Bob—"I am very happy!"

Mrs. Cratchit kissed him, his daughters kissed him, the two young Cratchits kissed him, and Peter and himself shook hands. Spirit of Tiny Tim, thy childish essence was from God!

"Specter," said Scrooge, "something informs me that our parting moment is at hand. I know it, but I know not how. Tell me what man that was whom we saw lying dead."

The Ghost of Christmas Yet to Come conveyed him, as before—

though at a different time, he thought; indeed, there seemed no order in these later visions, save that they were in the Future—into the resorts of business men, but showed him not himself. Indeed, the Spirit did not stay for anything, but went straight on, as to the end just now desired, until besought by Scrooge to tarry for a moment.

"This court," said Scrooge, "through which we hurry now is where my place of occupation is, and has been for a length of time. I see the house. Let me behold what I shall be, in days to come!"

The Spirit stopped; the hand was pointed elsewhere.

"The house is yonder," Scrooge exclaimed. "Why do you point away?"

The inexorable finger underwent no change.

Scrooge hastened to the window of his office, and looked in. It was an office still, but not his. The furniture was not the same, and the figure in the chair was not himself. The Phantom pointed as before.

He joined it once again, and, wondering why and whither he had gone, accompanied it until they reached an iron gate. He paused to look round before entering.

A churchyard. Here, then, the wretched man whose name he had now to learn lay underneath the ground. It was a worthy place. Walled in by houses, overrun by grass and weeds, the growth of vegetation's death, not life; choked up with too much burying, fat with repleted appetite. A worthy place!

The Spirit stood among the graves, and pointed down to One. He advanced toward it, trembling. The Phantom was exactly as it had been, but he dreaded that he saw new meaning in its solemn shape.

"Before I draw nearer to that stone to which you point," said Scrooge, "answer me one question. Are these the shadows of the things that Will be or are they shadows of the things that May be, only?"

Still the Ghost pointed downward to the grave by which it stood.

"Men's courses will foreshadow certain ends, to which, if persevered in, they must lead," said Scrooge. "But if the courses be departed from, the ends will change. Say it is thus with what you show me!"

The Spirit was immovable as ever.

Scrooge crept toward it, trembling as he went; and following the finger, read upon the stone of the neglected grave his own name, EBENEZER SCROOGE.

"Am *I* that man who lay upon the bed?" he cried, upon his knees.

The finger pointed from the grave to him, and back again.

"No, Spirit! Oh, no, no!"

The finger still was there.

"Spirit!" he cried, tight clutching at its robe, "hear me! I am not the man I was. I will not be the man I must have been but for this intercourse. Why show me this, if I am past all hope?"

For the first time the hand appeared to shake.

"Good Spirit," he pursued, as down upon the ground he fell before it, "your nature intercedes for me, and pities me. Assure me that I yet may change these shadows you have shown me, by an altered life!"

The kind hand trembled.

"I will honor Christmas in my heart, and try to keep it all the year. I will live in the Past, Present, and the Future. The Spirits of all Three shall strive within me. I will not shut out the lessons that they teach. Oh, tell me I may sponge away the writing on this stone!"

In his agony he caught the spectral hand. It sought to free itself, but he was strong in his entreaty, and detained it. The Spirit, stronger yet, repulsed him.

Holding up his hands in a last prayer to have his fate reversed, he saw an alteration in the Phantom's hood and dress. It shrunk, collapsed, and dwindled down into a bedpost.

Stave Five   The End of It

Yes! And the bedpost was his own. The bed was his own, the room was his own. Best and happiest of all, the Time before him was his own, to make amends in!

"I will live in the Past, the Present, and the Future!" Scrooge repeated, as he scrambled out of bed. "The Spirits of all Three shall strive within me. O Jacob Marley! Heaven and the Christmas-time be praised for this! I say it on my knees, old Jacob, on my knees!"

He was so fluttered and so glowing with his good intentions, that his broken voice would scarcely answer to his call. He had been sobbing violently in his conflict with the Spirit, and his face was wet with tears.

"They are not torn down," cried Scrooge, folding one of his bed-curtains in his arms—"they are not torn down rings and all. They are here—I am here—the shadows of the things that would have been may be dispelled. They will be. I know they will!"

His hands were busy with his garments all this time; turning them inside out, putting them on upside down, tearing them, mislaying them, making them parties to every kind of extravagance.

"I don't know what to do!" cried Scrooge, laughing and crying in the same breath, and making a perfect Laocoön of himself with his stockings. "I am as light as a feather, I am as happy as an angel, I am as merry as a schoolboy. I am as giddy as a drunken man. A merry Christmas to everybody! A happy New Year to all the world! Hallo here! Whoop! Hallo!"

He had frisked into the sitting-room, and was now standing there, perfectly winded.

"There's the saucepan that the gruel was in!" cried Scrooge, starting off again, and going round the fireplace. "There's the door by which the Ghost of Jacob Marley entered! There's the corner where the Ghost of Christmas Present sat! There's the window where I saw the wandering Spirits! It's all right, it's all true, it all happened. Ha, ha, ha!"

Really, for a man who had been out of practice for so many years, it was a splendid laugh, a most illustrious laugh. The father of a long, long line of brilliant laughs!

"I don't know what day of the month it is," said Scrooge. "I don't know how long I have been among the Spirits. I don't know anything. I'm quite a baby. Never mind. I don't care. I'd rather be a baby. Hallo! Whoop! Hallo here!"

He was checked in his transports by the churches ringing out the lustiest peals he had ever heard. Clash, clash, hammer; ding, dong, bell! Bell, dong, ding; hammer, clang, clash! Oh, glorious, glorious!

Running to the window, he opened it, and put out his head. No fog, no mist; clear, bright, jovial, stirring, cold; cold, piping for the blood to dance to; golden sunlight; heavenly sky; sweet fresh air; merry bells. Oh, glorious! Glorious!

"What's to-day?" cried Scrooge, calling downward to a boy in Sunday clothes, who perhaps had loitered in to look about him.

"Eh?" returned the boy, with all his might of wonder.

"What's to-day, my fine fellow?" said Scrooge.

"To-day!" replied the boy. "Why, *Christmas Day.*"

"It's Christmas Day!" said Scrooge to himself. "I haven't missed it. The Spirits have done it all in one night. They can do anything they like. Of course they can. Of course they can. Hallo, my fine fellow!"

"Hallo!" returned the boy.

"Do you know the poulterer's, in the next street but one, at the corner?" Scrooge inquired.

"I should hope I did," replied the lad.

"An intelligent boy!" said Scrooge. "A remarkable boy! Do you know whether they've sold the prize Turkey that was hanging up there?—Not the little prize Turkey, the big one?"

"What, the one as big as me?" returned the boy.

"What a delightful boy!" said Scrooge. "It's a pleasure to talk to him. Yes, my buck!"

"It's hanging there now," replied the boy.

"Is it?" said Scrooge. "Go and buy it."

"Walk-ER!" exclaimed the boy.

"No, no," said Scrooge. "I am in earnest. Go and buy it, and tell 'em to bring it here, that I may give them the directions where to take it. Come back with the man, and I'll give you a shilling. Come back with him in less than five minutes, and I'll give you half a crown!"

The boy was off like a shot. He must have had a steady hand at a trigger who could have got a shot off half so fast.

"I'll send it to Bob Cratchit's," whispered Scrooge, rubbing his hands, and splitting with a laugh. "He sha'n't know who sends it. It's twice the size of Tiny Tim. Joe Miller never made such a joke as sending it to Bob's will be!"

The hand in which he wrote the address was not a steady one, but write it he did, somehow, and went down-stairs to open the street door, ready for the coming of the poulterer's man. As he stood there, waiting his arrival, the knocker caught his eye.

"I shall love it as long as I live!" cried Scrooge, patting it with his hand. "I scarcely ever looked at it before. What an honest expression it has in its face! It's a wonderful knocker!—Here's the Turkey. Hallo! Whoop! How are you? Merry Christmas!"

It *was* a Turkey! He never could have stood upon his legs, that bird. He would have snapped 'em short off in a minute, like sticks of sealing-wax.

"Why, it's impossible to carry that to Camden Town," said Scrooge. "You must have a cab."

The chuckle with which he said this, and the chuckle with which he paid for the Turkey, and the chuckle with which he paid for the cab, and the chuckle with which he recompensed the boy, were only to be exceeded by the chuckle with which he sat down breathless in his chair again, and chuckled till he cried.

Shaving was not an easy task, for his hand continued to shake very much and shaving requires attention, even when you don't dance while you are at it. But if he had cut the end of his nose off, he would have put a piece of sticking-plaster over it, and been quite satisfied.

He dressed himself "all in his best," and at last got out into the streets. The people were by this time pouring forth, as he had seen them with the Ghost of Christmas Present; and walking with his hands behind him, Scrooge regarded every one with a delighted smile. He looked so irresistibly pleasant, in a word, that three or four good-humored fellows said, "Good morning, sir! A merry Christmas to you!" And Scrooge said often afterward, that of all the blithe sounds he had ever heard, those were the blithest in his ears.

He had not gone far, when, coming on toward him he beheld the portly gentleman who had walked into his counting-house the day before, and said, "Scrooge and Marley's, I believe?" It sent a pang across his heart to think how this old gentleman would look upon him when they met, but he knew what path lay straight before him, and he took it.

"My dear sir," said Scrooge, quickening his pace, and taking the old gentleman by both his hands, "how do you do? I hope you succeeded yesterday. It was very kind of you. A merry Christmas to you, sir!"

"Mr. Scrooge?"

"Yes," said Scrooge. "That is my name, and I fear it may not be pleasant to you. Allow me to ask your pardon. And will you have the

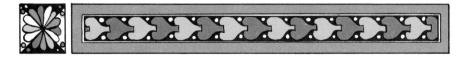

goodness—" Here Scrooge whispered in his ear.

"Lord bless me!" cried the gentleman, as if his breath were taken away. "My dear Mr. Scrooge, are you serious?"

"If you please," said Scrooge. "Not a farthing less. A great many back payments are included in it, I assure you. Will you do me that favor?"

"My dear sir," said the other, shaking hands with him, "I don't know what to say to such munifi—"

"Don't say anything, please," retorted Scrooge. "Come and see me. Will you come and see me?"

"I will!" cried the old gentleman. And it was clear he meant to do it.

"Thankee," said Scrooge. "I am much obliged to you. I thank you fifty times. Bless you!"

He went to church, and walked about the streets, and watched the people hurrying to and fro, and patted the children on the head, and questioned beggars, and looked down into the kitchens of houses, and up to the windows, and found that everything could yield him pleasure. He had never dreamed that any walk—that anything—could give him so much happiness. In the afternoon, he turned his steps toward his nephew's house.

He passed the door a dozen times before he had the courage to go up and knock. But he made a dash, and did it.

"Is your master at home, my dear?" said Scrooge to the girl. Nice girl! Very.

"Yes, sir."

"Where is he, my love?" said Scrooge.

"He's in the dining room, sir, along with mistress. I'll show you up-stairs, if you please."

"Thankee. He knows me," said Scrooge, with his hand already on the dining-room lock. "I'll go in here, my dear."

He turned it gently, and sidled his face in, round the door. They were looking at the table (which was spread out in great array); for these young house-keepers are always nervous on such points, and like to see that everything is right.

"Fred!" said Scrooge.

Dear heart alive, how his niece by marriage started! Scrooge had forgotten, for the moment, about her sitting in the corner with the

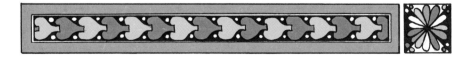

footstool, or he wouldn't have done it, on any account.

"Why, bless my soul!" cried Fred, "who's that?"

"It's I. Your uncle Scrooge. I have come to dinner. Will you let me in, Fred?"

Let him in! It is a mercy he didn't shake his arm off. He was at home in five minutes. Nothing could be heartier. His niece looked just the same. So did Topper, when *he* came. So did the plump sister, when *she* came. So did every one, when *they* came. Wonderful party, wonderful games, wonderful unanimity, won-der-ful happiness!

But he was early at the office next morning. Oh, he was early there! If he could only be there first, and catch Bob Cratchit coming late! That was the thing he had set his heart upon.

And he did it, yes, he did! The clock struck nine. No Bob. A quarter past. No Bob. He was full eighteen minutes and a half behind his time. Scrooge sat with his door wide open, that he might see him come into the tank.

His hat was off before he opened the door, his comforter, too. He was on his stool in a jiffy driving away with his pen, as if he were trying to overtake nine o'clock.

"Hallo!" growled Scrooge, in his accustomed voice as near as he could feign it. "What do you mean by coming here at this time of day?"

"I am very sorry, sir," said Bob. "I *am* behind my time."

"You are?" repeated Scrooge. "Yes. I think you are. Step this way, sir, if you please."

"It's only once a year, sir," pleaded Bob, appearing from the tank. "It shall not be repeated. I was making rather merry yesterday, sir."

"Now, I'll tell you what, my friend," said Scrooge, "I am not going to stand this sort of thing any longer. And therefore," he continued, leaping from his stool, and giving Bob such a dig in the waistcoat that he staggered back into the tank again—"and therefore, I am about to raise your salary!"

Bob trembled, and got a little nearer to the ruler. He had a momentary idea of knocking Scrooge down with it, holding him, and calling to the people in the court for help and a strait-waistcoat.

"A merry Christmas, Bob!" said Scrooge, with an earnestness that could not be mistaken, as he clapped him on the back. "A merrier Christmas, Bob, my good fellow, than I have given you for many a year! I'll raise your salary, and endeavor to assist your struggling family, and we will discuss your affairs this very afternoon, over a Christmas bowl of smoking bishop, Bob! Make up the fires, and buy another coal-scuttle before you dot another *i*, Bob Cratchit!"

Scrooge was better than his word. He did it all, and infinitely more; and to Tiny Tim, who did NOT die, he was a second father. He became as good a friend, as good a master, and as good a man as the good old City knew, or any other good old city, town, or borough in the good old world. Some people laughed to see the alteration in him, but he let them laugh, and little heeded them, for he was wise enough to know that nothing ever happened on this globe, for good, at which some people did not have their fill of laughter in the outset; and knowing that such as these would be blind anyway, he thought it quite as well that they should wrinkle up their eyes in grins, as have the malady in less attractive forms. His own heart laughed, and that was quite enough for him.

He had no further intercourse with Spirits, but lived upon the Total Abstinence Principle ever afterward; and it was always said of him, that he knew how to keep Christmas well, if any man alive possessed the knowledge. May that be truly said of us, and all of us! And so, as Tiny Tim observed, God Bless Us, Every One!

Charles Dickens

The Traditions

A CATCH BY THE HEARTH

Sing we all merrily
   Christmas is here,
The day that we love best
   Of days in the year.

Bring forth the holly,
   The box, and the bay,
Deck out our cottage
   For glad Christmas-day.

Sing we all merrily,
   Draw around the fire,
Sister and brother,
   Grandsire, and sire.
            Author Unknown

THE HOLLY AND THE IVY

From the Fifteenth Century

The Holly and the Ivy,
  When they are both full grown
Of all the trees are in the wood,
  The Holly bears the crown.

O the rising of the sun,
  And the running of the deer,
The playing of the merry organ,
  Sweet singing in the choir.

The Holly bears a blossom
  As white as any flower;
And Mary bore sweet Jesus Christ
  To be our sweet Saviour.

The Holly bears a berry
  As red as any blood;
And Mary bore sweet Jesus Christ
  To do poor sinners good.

The Holly bears a prickle
  As sharp as any thorn;
And Mary bore sweet Jesus Christ
  On Christmas in the morn.

The Holly bears a bark
  As bitter as any gall;
And Mary bore sweet Jesus Christ
  For to redeem us all.

The Holly and the Ivy
  Now both are full well grown:
Of all the trees are in the wood
  The Holly bears the crown.

JOLLY OLD SAINT NICHOLAS

Jolly old Saint Nicholas,
  Lean your ear this way!
Don't you tell a single soul
  What I'm going to say;
Christmas Eve is coming soon;
  Now you dear old man,
Whisper what you'll bring to me;
  Tell me if you can.

When the clock is striking twelve,
  When I'm fast asleep,
Down the chimney broad and black,
  With your pack you'll creep;
All the stockings you will find
  Hanging in a row;
Mine will be the shortest one,
  You'll be sure to know.

Johnny wants a pair of skates;
  Susy wants a sled;
Nellie wants a picture book;
  Yellow, blue and red;
Now I think I'll leave to you
  What to give the rest;
Choose for me, dear Santa Claus,
  You will know the best.

Old Song

HEART TO HEART

The years bring MANY CHANGES in MANY WAYS, it's true . . .
And perhaps I should change and "modernize" too . . . Perhaps I
should stop sending long Christmas rhymes . . . And change to a
greeting more in tune with the times . . . Something that's casual
and impersonally terse . . . Instead of a warm little "heart-to-heart"
verse . . . For I have been told that in this modern day . . . A "heart-
to-heart" greeting is strictly passé . . . But I can't help feeling there's
already too much . . . Of that heartlessly cold and impersonal touch
. . . In business and all walks of living today . . . And nothing remains
to "brighten our way" . . . For what is there left to make the heart
sing . . . When life is a cold and mechanical thing . . . And what have
we won if in reaching this goal . . . We gain the whole world and
lose our own soul . . . And so, though I'm open to much ridicule . . .
As one who belongs to an "outmoded school" . . . I still am con-
vinced that kindness, not force . . . Is the wiser and better and more
Christ-like course . . . For no modern world of controlled automation
. . . No matter how perfect its regimentation . . . Can ever bring joy
or peace to the earth . . . Or fulfill the promise of Jesus Christ's birth
. . . For progress, and money, and buttons to press . . . And comfort
and leisure and toil that is less . . . Cannot by themselves make a
world that is free . . . Where all live together in true harmony . . .
For it isn't the progress made by man's mind . . . But a sensitive heart
that is generous and kind . . . That can lighten life's burden and soften
life's sorrow . . . And open the way to a BETTER TOMORROW . . .
And a BETTER TOMORROW is my wish and my prayer . . . Not
only for you but for folks everywhere . . . And I hope that this
Christmas will bring you and yours . . . The joy that's eternal and
the peace that endures . . . But with LIFE'S MANY CHANGES one
fact remains true . . . I'm richer for having known SOMEONE LIKE
YOU.

Helen Steiner Rice

151

From PICKWICK PAPERS

From the centre of the ceiling . . . old Wardle had just suspended, with his own hands, a huge branch of mistletoe, and this same branch of mistletoe instantaneously gave rise to a scene of general and most delightful scrambling and confusion; in the midst of which Mr. Pickwick with a gallantry that would have done honour to a descendant of Lady Tollimglower herself, took the old lady by the hand, led her beneath the mystic branch, and saluted her in all courtesy and decorum. The old lady submitted to this piece of practical politeness with all the dignity which befitted so important and serious a solemnity, but the younger ladies not being so thoroughly imbued with a superstitious veneration for the custom: or imagining that the value of a salute is very much enhanced if it cost a little trouble to obtain it: screamed and struggled, and ran into corners, and threatened and remonstrated, and did everything but leave the room, until some of the less adventurous gentlemen were on the point of desisting, when they all at once found it useless to resist any longer, and submitted to be kissed with a good grace. Mr. Winkle kissed the young lady with the black eyes, and Mr. Snodgrass kissed Emily, and Mr. Weller, not being particular about the form of being under the mistletoe, kissed Emma and the other female servants, just as he caught them. As to the poor relations, they kissed everybody, not even excepting the plainer portions of the young-lady visitors, who, in their excessive confusion, ran right under the mistletoe as soon as it was hung up, without knowing it! Wardle stood with his back to the fire, surveying the whole scene, with the utmost satisfaction; and the fat boy took the opportunity of appropriating to his own use, and summarily devouring, a particularly fine mince-pie, that had been carefully put by for somebody else.

Now, the screaming had subsided, and faces were in a glow, and curls in a tangle, and Mr. Pickwick, after kissing the old lady as before mentioned, was standing under the mistletoe, looking with a very pleased countenance on all that was passing around him, when the young lady with the black eyes, after a little whispering with the other young ladies, made a sudden dart forward, and, putting her arm round Mr. Pickwick's neck, saluted him affectionately on the left cheek; and before Mr. Pickwick distinctly knew what was the matter, he was surrounded by the whole body, and kissed by every one of them.

Charles Dickens

for Santa only
Your friend,
Fred

THE POOR RELATION'S STORY

He was very reluctant to take precedence of so many respected members of the family, by beginning the round of stories they were to relate as they sat in a goodly circle by the Christmas fire; and he modestly suggested that it would be more correct if "John our esteemed host" (whose health he begged to drink) would have the kindness to begin. For as to himself, he said, he was so little used to lead the way that really— But as they all cried out here, that he must begin, and agreed with one voice that he might, could, would, and should begin, he left off rubbing his hands, and took his legs out from under his armchair, and did begin.

I have no doubt (said the poor relation) that I shall surprise the assembled members of our family, and particularly John our esteemed host, to whom we are so much indebted for the great hospitality with which he has this day entertained us, by the confession I am going to make. But, if you do me the honour to be surprised at anything that falls from a person so unimportant in the family as I am, I can only say that I shall be scrupulously accurate in all I relate.

I am not what I am supposed to be. I am quite another thing. Perhaps before I go further, I had better glance at what I *am* supposed to be.

It is supposed, unless I mistake—the assembled members of our family will correct me if I do, which is very likely (here the poor relation looked mildly about him for contradiction); that I am nobody's enemy but my own. That I never met with any particular success in anything. That I failed in business because I was unbusiness-like and credulous—in not being prepared for the interested designs of my partner. That I failed in love, because I was ridiculously trustful—in thinking it impossible that Christiana could deceive me. That I failed in my expectations from my uncle Chill, on account of not being as sharp as he could have wished in worldly matters. That, through life, I have been rather put upon and disappointed in a general way. That I am at present a bachelor of between fifty-nine and sixty years of age, living on a limited income in the form of a quarterly allowance, to which I see that John our esteemed host wishes me to make no further allusion.

The supposition as to my present pursuits and habits is to the following effect.

I live in a lodging in the Clapham Road—a very clean back room, in a very respectable house—where I am expected not to be at home in the day-time, unless poorly; and which I usually leave in the morning at nine o'clock, on pretence of going to business. I take my breakfast—my roll and butter, and my half-pint of coffee—at the old-established coffee-shop near Westminster Bridge; and then I go into the City—I don't know why—and sit in Garraway's Coffee House, and on 'Change, and walk about, and look into a few offices and counting-houses where some of my relations or acquaintance are so good as to tolerate me, and where I stand by the fire if the weather happens to be cold. I get through the day in this way until five o'clock, and then I dine: at a cost, on the average, of one and threepence. Having still a little money to spend on my evening's entertainment, I look into the old-established coffee-shop as I go home, and take my cup of tea, and perhaps my bit of toast. So, as the large hand of the clock makes its way round to the morning hour again, I make my way round to the Clapham Road again, and go to bed when I get to my lodging—fire being expensive, and being objected to by the family on account of its giving trouble and making a dirt.

Sometimes, one of my relations or acquaintance is so obliging as to ask me to dinner. These are holiday occasions, and then I generally walk in the Park. I am a solitary man, and seldom walk with anybody. Not that I am avoided because I am shabby; for I am not at all shabby, having always a very good suit of black on (or rather Oxford mixture, which has the appearance of black and wears much better); but I have got into a habit of speaking low, and being rather silent, and my spirits are not high, and I am sensible that I am not an attractive companion.

The only exception to this general rule is the child of my first cousin, Little Frank. I have a particular affection for that child, and he takes very kindly to me. He is a diffident boy by nature; and in a crowd he is soon run over, as I may say, and forgotten. He and I, however, get on exceedingly well. I have a fancy that the poor child will in time succeed to my peculiar position in the family. We talk but little; still, we understand each other. We walk about, hand in hand; and without much speaking he knows what I mean, and I know what he means. When he was very little indeed, I used to take him to the windows of the toy-shops, and show him the toys inside. It is surprising how soon he found out that I would have made him a great many presents if I had been in circumstances to do it.

Little Frank and I go and look at the outside of the Monument —he is very fond of the Monument—and at the Bridges, and at all the sights that are free. On two of my birthdays, we have dined on à-la-mode beef, and gone at half-price to the play, and been deeply interested. I was once walking with him in Lombard Street, which we often visit on account of my having mentioned to him that there are great riches there—he is very fond of Lombard Street—when a gentleman said to me as he passed by, "Sir, your little son has dropped his glove." I assure you, if you will excuse my remarking on so trivial a circumstance, this accidental mention of the child as mine, quite touched my heart and brought the foolish tears into my eyes.

When Little Frank is sent to school in the country, I shall be very much at a loss what to do with myself, but I have the intention of walking down there once a month and seeing him on a half-holiday. I am told he will then be at play upon the Heath; and if my visits should be objected to, as unsettling the child, I can see him from a distance without his seeing me, and walk back again. His

mother comes of a highly genteel family, and rather disapproves, I am aware, of our being too much together. I know that I am not calculated to improve his retiring disposition; but I think he would miss me beyond the feeling of the moment if we were wholly separated.

When I die in the Clapham Road, I shall not leave much more in this world than I shall take out of it; but, I happen to have a miniature of a bright-faced boy, with a curling head, and an open shirt-frill waving down his bosom (my mother had it taken for me, but I can't believe that it was ever like), which will be worth nothing to sell, and which I shall beg may be given to Frank. I have written my dear boy a little letter with it, in which I have told him that I felt very sorry to part from him, though bound to confess that I know no reason why I should remain here. I have given him some short advice, the best in my power, to take warning of the consequences of being nobody's enemy but his own; and I have endeavoured to comfort him for what I fear he will consider a bereavement, by pointing out to him, that I was only a superfluous something to every one but him; and that having by some means failed to find a place in this great assembly, I am better out of it.

Such (said the poor relation, clearing his throat and beginning to speak a little louder) is the general impression about me. Now, it is a remarkable circumstance which forms the aim and purpose of my story, that this is all wrong. This is not my life, and these are not my habits. I do not even live in the Clapham Road. Comparatively speaking, I am very seldom there. I reside, mostly, in a—I am almost ashamed to say the word, it sounds so full of pretension—in a Castle. I do not mean that it is an old baronial habitation, but still it is a building always known to every one by the name of a Castle. In it, I preserve the particulars of my history; they run thus:

It was when I first took John Spatter (who had been my clerk) into partnership, and when I was still a young man of not more than five-and twenty, residing in the house of my uncle Chill, from whom I had considerable expectations, that I ventured to propose to Christiana. I had loved Christiana a long time. She was very beautiful, and very winning in all respects. I rather mistrusted her widowed mother, who I feared was of a plotting and mercenary turn of mind; but, I thought as well of her as I could, for Christiana's sake. I never had loved any one but Christiana, and she had been all the world, and oh, far more than all the world, to me, from our childhood!

Christiana accepted me with her mother's consent, and I was rendered very happy indeed. My life at my uncle Chill's was of a spare dull kind, and my garret chamber was as dull, and bare, and cold, as an upper prison room in some stern northern fortress. But, having Christiana's love, I wanted nothing upon earth. I would not have changed my lot with any human being.

Avarice was, unhappily, my uncle Chill's master-vice. Though he was rich, he pinched, and scraped, and clutched, and lived miserably. As Christiana had no fortune, I was for some time a little fearful of confessing our engagement to him; but, at length I wrote him a letter, saying how it all truly was. I put it into his hand one night, on going to bed.

As I came downstairs next morning, shivering in the cold December air; colder in my uncle's unwarmed house than in the street, where the winter sun did sometimes shine, and which was at all events enlivened by cheerful faces and voices passing along; I carried a heavy heart towards the long, low breakfast-room in which my uncle sat. It was a large room with a small fire, and there was a great bay window in it which the rain had marked in the night as if with the tears of houseless people. It stared upon a raw yard, with a cracked stone pavement, and some rusted iron railings half uprooted, whence an ugly outbuilding that had once been a dissecting-room (in the time of the great surgeon who had mortgaged the house to my uncle), stared at it.

We rose so early always, that at that time of the year we break-fasted by candlelight. When I went into the room, my uncle was so contracted by the cold, and so huddled together in his chair behind the one dim candle, that I did not see him until I was close to the table.

As I held out my hand to him, he caught up his stick (being infirm, he always walked about the house with a stick), and made a blow at me, and said, "You fool!"

"Uncle," I returned, "I didn't expect you to be so angry as this." Nor had I expected it, though he was a hard and angry old man.

"You didn't expect!" said he; "when did you ever expect? When did you ever calculate, or look forward, you contemptible dog?"

"These are hard words, Uncle!"

"Hard words? Feathers, to pelt such an idiot as you with," said he. "Here! Betsy Snap! Look at him!"

Betsy Snap was a withered, hard-featured, yellow old woman—our only domestic—always employed, at this time of the morning, in rubbing my uncle's legs. As my uncle adjured her to look at me, he put his lean grip on the crown of her head, she kneeling beside him, and turned her face towards me. An involuntary thought connecting them both with the dissecting-room, as it must often have been in the surgeon's time, passed across my mind in the midst of my anxiety.

"Look at the snivelling milksop!" said my uncle. "Look at the baby! This is the gentleman who, people say, is nobody's enemy but his own. This is the gentleman who can't say no. This is the gentleman

159

who was making such large profits in his business that he must needs take a partner, t'other day. This is the gentleman who is going to marry a wife without a penny, and who falls into the hands of Jezebels who are speculating on my death!"

I knew, now, how great my uncle's rage was; for nothing short of his being almost beside himself would have induced him to utter that concluding word, which he held in such repugnance that it was never spoken or hinted at before him on any account.

"On my death," he repeated, as if he were defying me by defying his own abhorrence of the word. "On my death—death—Death! But I'll spoil the speculation. Eat your last under this roof, you feeble wretch, and may it choke you!"

You may suppose that I had not much appetite for the breakfast to which I was bidden in these terms; but, I took my accustomed seat. I saw that I was repudiated henceforth by my uncle; still I could bear that very well, possessing Christiana's heart.

He emptied his basin of bread-and-milk as usual, only that he took it on his knees with his chair turned away from the table where I sat. When he had done, he carefully snuffed out the candle; and the cold, slate-coloured, miserable day looked in upon us.

"Now, Mr. Michael," said he, "before we part, I should like to have a word with these ladies in your presence."

"As you will, sir," I returned; "but you deceive yourself, and wrong us, cruelly, if you suppose that there is any feeling at stake in this contract but pure, disinterested, faithful love."

To this, he only replied, "You lie!" and not one other word.

We went, through half-thawed snow and half-frozen rain, to the house where Christiana and her mother lived. My uncle knew them very well. They were sitting at their breakfast, and were surprised to see us at that hour.

"Your servant, ma'am," said my uncle to the mother. "You divine the purpose of my visit, I dare say, ma'am. I understand there is a world of pure, disinterested, faithful love cooped up here. I am happy to bring it all it wants, to make it complete. I bring you your son-in-law, ma'am—and you, your husband, miss. The gentleman is a perfect stranger to me, but I wish him joy of his wise bargain."

He snarled at me as he went out, and I never saw him again.

It is altogether a mistake (continued the poor relation) to suppose that my dear Christiana, over-persuaded and influenced by her mother, married a rich man, the dirt from whose carriage-wheels is often, in these changed times, thrown upon me as she rides by. No, no. She married me.

The way we came to be married rather sooner than we intended was this. I took a frugal lodging and was saving and planning for her sake, when, one day, she spoke to me with great earnestness, and said:

"My dear Michael, I have given you my heart. I have said that I loved you, and I have pledged myself to be your wife. I am as much yours through all changes of good and evil as if we had been married on the day when such words passed between us. I know you well, and know that if we should be separated and our union broken off, your whole life would be shadowed, and all that might, even now, be stronger in your character for the conflict with the world would then be weakened to the shadow of what it is!"

"God help me, Christiana!" said I. "You speak the truth."

"Michael!" said she, putting her hand in mine, in all maidenly devotion, "let us keep apart no longer. It is but for me to say that I can live contented upon such means as you have, and I well know you are happy. I say so from my heart. Strive no more alone; let us strive together. My dear Michael, it is not right that I should keep secret from you what you do not suspect, but what distresses my whole life. My mother: without considering that what you have lost, you have lost for me, and on the assurance of my faith: sets her heart on riches, and urges another suit upon me, to my misery. I cannot bear this, for to bear it is to be untrue to you. I would rather share your struggles than look on. I want no better home than you can give me. I know that you will aspire and labour with a higher courage if I am wholly yours, and let it be so when you will!"

I was blest indeed, that day, and a new world opened to me. We were married in a very little while, and I took my wife to our happy home. That was the beginning of the residence I have spoken of; the Castle we have ever since inhabited together, dates from that time. All our children have been born in it. Our first child—now married—was a little girl, whom we called Christiana. Her son is so like

Little Frank, that I hardly know which is which.

The current impression as to my partner's dealings with me is also quite erroneous. He did not begin to treat me coldly, as a poor simpleton, when my uncle and I so fatally quarrelled; nor did he afterwards gradually possess himself of our business and edge me out. On the contrary, he behaved to me with the utmost good faith and honour.

Matters between us took this turn: On the day of my separation from my uncle, and even before the arrival at our counting-house of my trunks (which he sent after me, *not* carriage paid), I went down to our room of business, on our little wharf, overlooking the river; and there I told John Spatter what had happened. John did not say, in reply, that rich old relatives were palpable facts, and that love and sentiment were moonshine and fiction. He addressed me thus:

"Michael," said John, "we were at school together, and I generally had the knack of getting on better than you, and making a higher reputation."

"You had, John," I returned.

"Although," said John, "I borrowed your books and lost them; borrowed your pocket-money, and never repaid it; got you to buy my damaged knives at a higher price than I had given for them new; and to own to the windows that I had broken."

"All not worth mentioning, John Spatter," said I, "but certainly true."

"When you were first established in this infant business, which promises to thrive so well," pursued John, "I came to you, in my search for almost any employment, and you made me your clerk."

"Still not worth mentioning, my dear John Spatter," said I; "still, equally true."

"And finding that I had a good head for business, and that I was really useful *to* the business, you did not like to retain me in that capacity, and thought it an act of justice soon to make me your partner."

"Still less worth mentioning than any of those other little circumstances you have recalled, John Spatter," said I; "for I was, and am, sensible of your merits and my deficiencies."

"Now, my good friend," said John, drawing my arm through his, as he had had a habit of doing at school; while two vessels outside the windows of our counting-house—which were shaped like the stern windows of a ship—went lightly down the river with the tide, as John and I might then be sailing away in company, and in trust and confidence, on our voyage of life; "let there, under these friendly circumstances, be a right understanding between us. You are too easy, Michael. You are nobody's enemy but your own. If I were to give you that damaging character among our connexion, with a shrug, and a shake of the head, and a sigh; and if I were further to abuse the trust you place in me—"

"But you never will abuse it at all, John," I observed.

"Never!" said he; "but I am putting a case—I say, and if I were further to abuse that trust by keeping this piece of our common affairs in the dark, and this other piece in the light, and again this other piece in the twilight, and so on, I should strengthen my strength, and weaken your weakness, day by day, until at last I found myself on the high road to fortune, and you left behind on some bare common, a hopeless number of miles out of the way."

"Exactly so," said I.

"To prevent this, Michael," said John Spatter, "or the remotest chance of this, there must be perfect openness between us. Nothing must be concealed, and we must have but one interest."

"My dear John Spatter," I assured him, "that is precisely what I mean."

"And when you are too easy," pursued John, his face glowing with friendship, "you must allow me to prevent that imperfection in your nature from being taken advantage of, by any one; you must not expect me to humour it—"

"My dear John Spatter," I interrupted, "I *don't* expect you to humour it. I want to correct it."

"And I, too," said John.

"Exactly so!" cried I. "We both have the same end in view; and, honourably seeking it, and fully trusting one another, and having but one interest, ours will be a prosperous and happy partnership."

"I am sure of it!" returned John Spatter. And we shook hands most affectionately.

I took John home to my Castle, and we had a very happy day. Our partnership throve very well. My friend and partner supplied what I wanted, as I had foreseen that he would; and by improving both the business and myself, amply acknowledged any little rise in life to which I had helped him.

I am not (said the poor relation, looking at the fire as he slowly rubbed his hands) very rich, for I never cared to be that; but I have enough, and am above all moderate wants and anxieties. My Castle is not a splendid place, but it is very comfortable, and it has a warm and cheerful air, and is quite a picture of Home.

Our eldest girl, who is very like her mother, married John Spatter's eldest son. Our two families are closely united in other areas of attachment. It is very pleasant of an evening, when we are all assembled together—which frequently happens—and when John and I talk over old times, and the one interest there has always been between us.

I really do not know, in my Castle, what loneliness is. Some of our children or grandchildren are always about it, and the young voices of my descendants are delightful—oh, how delightful!—to me to hear. My dearest and most devoted wife, ever faithful, ever loving, ever helpful and sustaining and consoling, is the priceless blessing of my house; from whom all its other blessings spring. We are rather a musical family, and when Christiana sees me, at any time, a little weary or depressed, she steals to the piano and sings a gentle air she used to sing when we were first betrothed. So weak a man am I, that I cannot bear to hear it from any other source. They played it once, at the Theatre, when I was there with Little Frank; and the child said wondering, "Cousin Michael, whose hot tears are these that have fallen on my hand?"

Such is my Castle, and such are the real particulars of my life therein preserved. I often take Little Frank home there. He is very welcome to my grandchildren, and they play together. At this time of the year—the Christmas and New Year time—I am seldom out of my Castle. For, the associations of the season seem to hold me there, and the precepts of the season seem to teach me that it is well to be there.

"And the Castle is—" observed a grave, kind voice among the company.

"Yes. My Castle," said the poor relation, shaking his head as he still looked at the fire, "is in the Air. John our esteemed host suggests its situation accurately. My Castle is in the Air! I have done. Will you be so good as to pass the story!"

Charles Dickens

A VISIT FROM ST. NICHOLAS

'Twas the night before Christmas, when all through the house
Not a creature was stirring, not even a mouse.
The stockings were hung by the chimney with care,
In hopes that St. Nicholas soon would be there.
The children were nestled all snug in their beds,
While visions of sugar-plums danced in their heads;
And mamma in her kerchief, and I in my cap,
Had just settled our brains for a long winter's nap—
When out on the lawn there arose such a clatter
I sprang from my bed to see what was the matter.
Away to the window I flew like a flash,
Tore open the shutter, and threw up the sash.
The moon on the breast of the new-fallen snow
Gave a lustre of midday to objects below;
When what to my wondering eye should appear
But a miniature sleigh and eight tiny reindeer,
With a little old driver, so lively and quick,
I knew in a moment it must be St. Nick!
More rapid than eagles his coursers they came,
And he whistled and shouted and called them by name.
"Now, Dasher! now, Dancer! now, Prancer and Vixen!
On, Comet! on, Cupid! on, Donder and Blitzen!—
To the top of the porch, to the top of the wall,
Now, dash away, dash away, dash away all!"
As dry leaves that before the wild hurricane fly,
When they meet with an obstacle mount to the sky,
So, up to the housetop the coursers they flew,
With a sleigh full of toys—and St. Nicholas, too.
And then, in a twinkling, I heard on the roof
The prancing and pawing of each little hoof.
As I drew in my head and was turning around,
Down the chimney St. Nicholas came with a bound:
He was dressed all in fur from his head to his foot,
And his clothes were all tarnished with ashes and soot:
A bundle of toys he had flung on his back,
And he looked like a peddler just opening his pack.

His eyes, how they twinkled! his dimples, how merry!
His cheeks were like roses, his nose like a cherry;
His droll little mouth was drawn up like a bow,
And the beard on his chin was as white as the snow.
The stump of a pipe he held tight in his teeth,
And the smoke, it encircled his head like a wreath.
He had a broad face and a little round belly
That shook, when he laughed, like a bowl full of jelly.
He was chubby and plump—a right jolly old elf:
And I laughed when I saw him, in spite of myself;
A wink of his eye, and a twist of his head,
Soon gave me to know I had nothing to dread.
He spoke not a word, but went straight to his work,
And filled all the stockings: then turned with a jerk,
And laying his finger aside of his nose,
And giving a nod, up the chimney he rose.
He sprang to his sleigh, to his team gave a whistle,
And away they all flew like the down of a thistle.
But I heard him exclaim, ere they drove out of sight,
"Happy Christmas to all, and to all a good-night!"

Clement Clarke Moore

WHAT SHALL WE DO THIS CHRISTMAS? *

We were in Scotland, my husband and I, and away from home at
Christmastime for the first time in our lives. It was December, 1953.
We had been married three years and Louie was studying at the
University of Edinburgh. Our first child, Danny, had been born two
months ago—just a few weeks after we arrived in Scotland—and he
made us a family—but such a small one!

My husband and I were accustomed to large family gatherings
at Christmas and we were beginning to feel the loneliness that comes
to those who are among unfamiliar faces and surroundings at a time
of the year when the familiar is deeply recalled—and needed. It
wouldn't be the same for us this year. Much as we loved Scotland
and were warmed by the people we met, they weren't "family," in
the traditional sense.

Before we were married we each spent the holidays at home among friends and relatives who came to be with us. Louie's family was large and mine was small, but our numbers always swelled at Christmas. And during the days before Christmas we knew the excitement of the familiar preparations—choosing the tree, unwrapping the ornaments, remembering the words to the lovely carols, the warm embrace of friends, the sudden, unguarded smiles from strangers passing on the street or in the stores, baking the pies for Christmas dinner, wrapping the presents. . . . These were our traditions. These were the things we always did. This was the way Christmas always was for us . . . and these customs gave us a secure, comfortable feeling of being able to hold onto the familiar in a world that was always new and different.

After we were married we spent Christmas day with my parents, and Louie's parents went to the home of one of his sisters. But still the traditions were kept intact and the familiar, lovable faces were there . . . and it was fun, fun, fun!

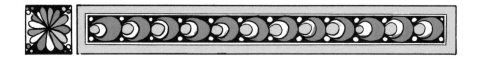

"What shall we do at Christmas *this* year?" we asked ourselves as we began to feel the first pangs of hunger for our families. No answer.

In Scotland we were foreign students, and as such we were invited to an international student party where we met some delightful young men and women from many different countries. They, too, were away from home and familiar faces. We felt especially drawn to two students from Nigeria—Sam and his beautiful cousin Iba. In the days following the party we saw quite a lot of them and got to know them very well. And then, one day when the question, "What shall we do at Christmas?" came up, the answer was obvious. Invite Sam and Iba to spend the day with us! Just because we weren't back home in the familiar surroundings, keeping the old traditions, sharing the day with our family-family, that didn't mean we had to be alone. Right outside our door there was another family that extended throughout the whole world . . . there were people who needed to be included in our lives just as much as we needed to have them with us. Sam and Iba—and any of their friends who didn't have a place to go on Christmas day—they were our heart-family!

On the three other Christmases we had spent as a married couple, my parents were the ones who did everything for me. They prepared the dinner and opened their house to us . . . and during all the other earlier years of my life I had been poured into by those who loved and cared for me. . . . I had been the child receiving, but now it was different . . . I was the woman whose privilege it was to provide, to prepare. I loved the feeling of it!

And prepare I did. I wanted to blend as many of our cultural traditions into the newness of our situation as I possibly could. We had a tree—a small one—decorated with a few ornaments I bought at the five-and-ten. Louie supplied the wood for our fireplace and we had a crackling fire burning all day, which thoroughly delighted our little son. I tried to collect the ingredients for a typical American Christmas dinner, but since some items were scarce (the war was not long over) I had to improvise. For instance, I couldn't get sweet potatoes, so I cooked carrots in large chunks and baked them with brown sugar.

We spent Christmas day in 1953 with our heart-family—Sam

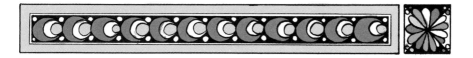

and Iba and a room full of other students who came in their colorful native dress. It was a wonderful day, one I shall never forget. We read the Christmas story from Matthew and Luke and we sang carols and laughed and embraced and shared the deep joy we felt in the knowledge that we were children of God. The Nigerians were such lively, animated people who spoke so openly of their love for Christ . . . and it was this love which bound us together, making us truly brothers and sisters of one another. And then I understood what Jesus meant when he said, "Who is my brother and my sister? These people are, those who do the will of God." Sam and Iba and their wonderful friends were *our* friends now . . . they were new to my life . . . they were not part of my past . . . they were not the familiar faces I had longed to see at Christmas—but they were part of my present and part of my future. And they were our family!

Because we were unable to keep our traditional Christmas that year, we spent it in untraditional ways . . . and we discovered that it is more important to keep the spirit of Christmas than to keep the customs with which we have grown up. Yes, we still love the traditions and keep them whenever we can, and we love to be with our family-family whenever we can . . . but we are grateful for the times when this was not possible, for the times when we couldn't be with our relatives and friends—and yet Christmas still happened . . . and in a most spirit-warming way.

Sometimes life doesn't come to us . . . sometimes we have to reach out for it. People won't always come to us . . . and instead of sitting home, waiting for someone to arrive . . . succumbing to the loneliness that comes to all of us when we are not with those who care for us, we have to reach out to those we need. Instead of asking ourselves, "Who's going to invite me for dinner?" why not ask, "Whom can I cook dinner for?"

After we returned from Scotland we began to form our own Christmas traditions as a family. Instead of going to my parents, we had them with us in our home, first in Bel Air and then in La Jolla, California, where Louie was called to serve two wonderful churches. As our children grew up they looked forward to these special gatherings each year. There were six of us now in our nuclear family—Louie and I, and our four children, Dan, Tim, Andie and Jim—and

at Christmastime our house was filled with friends as well as relatives
. . . and that was the only place in the world where we wanted to
be on that day.

A few years ago my husband received a call to National Presby-
terian Church in Washington, D.C., and we knew that that year
would be our last in La Jolla. Our family gathering would be especially dear to us, for we would carry its memories for a long, long
time.

And then we learned that my parents—Grandma and Grandpa
Wilhelm—would not be with us. Grandpa had to undergo surgery
and would have to spend Christmas day in a hospital north of Los
Angeles. So we mailed our gifts to each other and bit our lips a little
in our disappointment.

If it had been just Louie and I at Christmas I would have
suggested driving up to Los Angeles and spending the day with
Grandpa, but I just couldn't ask our children to do that. The trip
took three-and-a-half hours each way, which meant that we would
have to be away from home all day, and our sons and daughter so
enjoyed being home at Christmas. I knew their friends would be
dropping in all day—and that soon our children would be saying
good-bye to these friends for at least a long time. So I put the idea
out of my mind.

On Christmas morning we did what we always did as a family.
We got up very early, had a light breakfast and then we sat around
the tree while one of us read the Christmas story from the gospels.
Then we opened our presents, hugging and kissing each other for the
thoughtfulness and remembered wishes we found wrapped up in the
packages. But it wasn't the same without Grandma and Grandpa.
We missed them very much. Our tall, long-haired boys were touch-
ingly open about their feelings . . . "I sure miss Grandpa . . ." "He's
so much fun! . . ." "Yeah—he's a real cruiser! . . ." and Andie's
sensitive face and the sadness in her large compassionate eyes said
more than words.

It was time for me to take the turkey out of the refrigerator and
put it in the oven, and I was glad to have an excuse to go into the
kitchen because I thought I was going to cry a little. And I honestly